DIY FOR RENTERS

Don't Call the Landlord

A Renter's Guide to Repairs and Personalizations That Won't Break Your Lease

Charles Byers

CREATIVE
HOMEOWNER®

CRE▲TIVE
HOMEOWNER®

DIY for Renters: Don't Call the Landlord
Editor: Anthony Regolino
Designer: David Fisk
Indexer: Jay Kreider

ISBN 978-1-58011-833-0

The Cataloging-in-Publication Data is on file with the Library of Congress.

We are always looking for talented authors. To submit an idea, please send a brief inquiry to acquisitions@foxchapelpublishing.com.

Printed in Malaysia

Current Printing (last digit)
10 9 8 7 6 5 4 3 2 1

Creative Homeowner®, *www.creativehomeowner.com*, is an imprint of New Design Originals Corporation and distributed exclusively in North America by Fox Chapel Publishing Company, Inc., 800-457-9112, 903 Square Street, Mount Joy, PA 17552, and in the United Kingdom by Grantham Book Service, Trent Road, Grantham, Lincolnshire, NG31 7XQ.

DEDICATION

This book is dedicated to my wife, Rhonda Byers; my oldest daughter, Kimberly; my son, TJ; and my younger daughter, Courtney, all of whom have, in one way or another, contributed to my success in being the craftsman I am today.

Each has sacrificed, accepting my absence at sporting events, family meals, and weekend adventures because I was required to be on the job, creating finished projects for my customers. Being a small-town small business doesn't always afford the luxuries of a large staff of employees.

Each one of my family members has laid his or her own hand on a project by helping carry lumber, building some part, pulling wires, or just sitting on the roof, handing Dad shingles to be nailed in place. Their agreement to be part of a small business wasn't completely voluntary, but I think they have memories that they will never forget—even if it was being the object of a good practical joke on the site!

Lastly, to my father, Charles L. Byers, who was as instrumental in the success of a small construction company as I was, for he was my investment partner. He once asked me, "What major part did I play in the building of any of our projects?" To which I replied, "Your signature along with mine at our bank makes the materials and subcontractors possible to create the project." Without that, we would have just been two guys, wishing we were builders! We not only shared a small business venture but a great friendship as well. He passed in 1997 at the age of seventy-nine.

CONTENTS

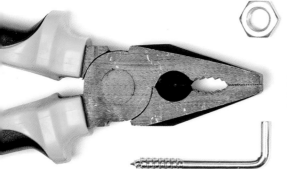

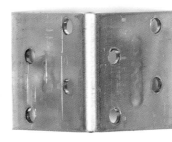

INTRODUCTION

DIY for Renters is a comprehensive list of items a tenant can expect to encounter while occupying a property. The list of projects, accompanied by detailed descriptions and photographs, will help the tenant with novice experience to identify the problem, as well as the experienced handyman, who will want to make the repair after checking with the property owner and obtaining permission.

The illustrations and descriptions in this book for each task are intended to inform the person what the problem may be and provide a simple plan and list of parts necessary to accomplish the repair. This book is not intended to be a manual for construction and remodeling projects or major repairs.

In most municipalities, the repairs listed in this book are intended to be direct replacement parts and procedures. Therefore, being part of repair processes rather than construction processes, these would fall outside of the realm of the building-permit process. Anything required beyond the items of repair in this book or behind the finished wall/ceiling surface would require the property owner to hire a professional contractor who is licensed and insured to perform the required repairs and obtain the necessary inspections of the completed work.

Whether the task is to replace a leaking P-trap washer under a bathroom vanity sink or troubleshoot a water-heater element to determine its condition, you must use the same mind-set to be successful; you must determine what the real problem (cause) is and what is required to repair it (solution) so that you can achieve the end result with the least amount of money and time.

Property owners today understand that their tenants are more informed and have at their availability a wealth of information to enable them to accurately communicate issues with the properties they are leasing. Gone are the days when a property owner could state that the problem is not what the tenant is describing or convince the tenant that there is nothing to be concerned about.

Another advantage that tenants have today is that they can use their smartphones to take photos or videos and send the images immediately to the property owners to further explain the issues and communicate their needs. Also, let's not forget the power of texting issues and concerns to the property owner.

Property owners understand that many tenants can do simple repairs. The best advice on this subject is to always consult with the property owner and your written lease agreement to be sure you are permitted to perform minor repairs. Many property owners will compensate their tenants for the materials because the materials remain with the property. Some may go as far as compensating the tenant for some labor costs because the cost of a contractor's service call alone could be much greater than the cost of a simple part and an hour of the tenant's labor. Some property owners may credit the next month's rent payment with the amount of the repair cost, previously agreed upon by owner and tenant. It is not acceptable to make a repair without prearrangement with the property owner unless you are willing to absorb the costs of the parts and provide free labor for the repair.

A lot can be said for good owner–tenant relations. A property owner takes the risk of owning a building that someone else will be occupying over an agreed-upon initial lease period, and then the lease usually converts to a year-to-year lease period thereafter. When the tenants enjoy the neighborhood and the property meets their needs, it is not uncommon for them to lease for extended periods of many years. This situation gives the property owner the security of a steady rental income and the tenant the opportunity to become part of the neighborhood and establish long-term friendships.

Skill Levels Explained

 BASIC is for those who are comfortable following directions and possess the ability to use hand tools.

 SEMISKILLED is for those who are comfortable with the Basic skill level and are able to extend that level to that of simple part replacements and the ability to use power tools.

 SKILLED is for those who are comfortable with the Semiskilled level and are able to extend that level to the more intricate disassembly and part replacements and the ability to use the most complex power tools.

CHAPTER 1

BEFORE YOU BEGIN

SAFETY FIRST

Read, follow, and exercise safety rules when working with all tools, both power and hand tools. Nothing spells "careless" more than inflicting a simple injury on yourself and having to be driven to the urgent care clinic for stitches!

■ Maintain all of your tools in safe working condition. Using a screwdriver as a chisel will only damage the plastic handle from repeated blows with a claw hammer. Chisel handles are made of a high-impact resin, and many have reinforced metal ends to sustain repeated hammer blows.

■ Use safety glasses when performing all work. You can't imagine the pain of having a piece of ceiling tile stuck inside your eye socket. Another example is the tiniest splinter from a plywood sheet that you are cutting, and it won't wash out of your eye. The doctor at the ER at 3:00 the next morning claims "that must have felt like a telephone pole in there!"

■ Maintain a safe work site. The use of battery-operated tools has greatly reduced the clutter of tangled cords. When you require more than one corded tool, I recommend using a multiple-socket power strip or extension cords with multiple sockets to eliminate pulling and reinstalling plugs from different tools. Your back will thank you also!

■ Electrical connections of power tools, lights, and air compressors must be connected to a GFCI receptacle or protected circuit using a three-prong extension cord to prevent electrical shock. Power tools today are required to be double-insulated, replacing the older metal-cased power tools that are now perceived as unsafe. This will reduce the danger of you or someone else being shocked while standing on an aluminum ladder with wet shoes from walking across the front lawn's morning dew.

When using stepladders, always face your work head-on.

Do not disregard warning labels.

- Ladders and elevated surfaces must be given special attention. The number-one cause of injuries related to construction or repair tasks is falls. Use ladders only for the sole purpose for which they were designed. Every day, someone uses a stepladder leaning against a wall as if it were an extension ladder. This can be extremely dangerous if the bottom of the ladder slides away from the wall. When using stepladders, always face your work head-on. Too many people set up the stepladder and then work to the side, which creates an out-of-balance situation.

- Another often-made mistake is ignoring the warning labels on the stepladder rungs. When it says "Do not stand on or above this surface," just get a taller ladder! Also, stepladder tops are often made with slots for holding tools and small recesses for holding parts; thus, you must take care not to be struck by falling objects when moving a stepladder.

- Clothes that you select to keep you safe go a long way. If you're working on a repair using a rotary tool while still wearing a necktie or identification lanyard from work, you can suffer profound injuries. Likewise, don't wear tennis shoes or other thin-soled shoes when outside digging a hole for the mailbox that was run over by the delivery truck; instead, wear hard-soled boots. Each time you work, you must ask yourself, "Am I wearing the best clothes to keep me safe and prevent me from getting hurt?"

Safety is a mind-set and a priority for everyone who works in the construction or repair industry. Utility companies spend weeks training their crews how to properly set ladders and operate bucket trucks. The Occupational Safety and Health Administration (OSHA) has covered every work discipline from mining to construction to set standards for safety and health-management procedures to make sure everyone has the same chance of working without injury or illness. Information on workplace safety can be found at www.osha.gov.

TIPS FOR SUCCESSFUL REPAIRS

- Plan to do your work when you have adequate time to do the repair right. Rushing can only add to the frustration level if you buy the wrong part or, worse, realize that a piece is missing from the package when you open it after returning from the home-supply center.
- Searching the website of the home-supply center you are going to visit can be extremely beneficial. Not only can you source the exact piece you need, you can compare prices and availability among different centers. You can also research to see if other parts might be listed as a clever idea to replace in addition to the one you think is bad.
- Call ahead to the home-supply center to be sure they have the exact part you are looking for. They might not remove one from their stock to reserve it for you at the service desk, but they might!
- Take the part or as much of it as you can to the home-supply center to match it correctly. A 1½-inch trap washer looks a lot like a 1¼-inch trap washer until you have the original to compare the new one to. It is also advisable to establish a rapport with the person working in the department from which you are buying parts at the home-supply center. Chances are they have experience helping other customers like you complete a project or have worked in the respective trade with which you are seeking help.
- Pictures are worth a thousand words. It can be extremely helpful to take pictures of your area of repair to take with you to the home-supply center. The person working there can often offer multiple solutions to your repair problem, possibly saving you time and expense. If only the J-bend portion of a corroded P-trap needs to be replaced, he or she can show you where that specific piece is located versus the complete P-trap assembly.
- Follow the manufacturer's supplied assembly and installation instructions explicitly. It would be awful to find out the #8-32 x 1-inch pan-head screw left over was supposed to be installed during step 1 of the assembly process, and you have to undo the complete assembly to install that screw! Don't believe for a minute it's just an extra piece they packed in the parts bag!
- Receipts are key to being able to return any incorrect or excess items that you have purchased. Receipts also may be required by the property owner for reimbursement to you. You can use receipts as reference tools for looking up items on the home-supply center's website before you go back to return something. By looking up the item numbers from the receipt, you will be able to tell which item is the correct one and which is the one you need to return. I can't tell you how many times I wanted **Part A** from **Bin A** only to have someone throw **Part B** in there prior—and guess who got **Part B** from **Bin A**?

Using these tips helps obtain the right parts to complete your repair and do it safely and efficiently so you can get back to the important things in life. Oh, and now you don't have to listen to that water drip falling into the bucket you placed under the leaking P-trap in the bathroom vanity anymore!

Tips for Successful Repairs

CHAPTER 2

DRYWALL ISSUES

DRYWALL REPAIRS BEFORE SPACKLING

SKILL LEVEL

- **Semiskilled**

TOOLS REQUIRED

- **Four-way screwdriver**
- **Pencil**
- **Tape measure**
- **Utility knife**
- **Torpedo level**
- **Drywall T-square**
- **Cordless screw gun**
- **4-inch taping knife**
- **Drywall jab saw**

MATERIALS REQUIRED

- **Drywall sheet of correct thickness (½-inch or ⅝-inch)**
- **Scrap wood**
- **1⅝-inch drywall screws**
- **Self-stick mesh joint tape**

Drywall damage can be found in all areas of a house, from something as simple as moving wall decorations and pictures. Don't forget the small damage caused by little children riding their tricycles in the house, going back and forth between living room, dining room, and kitchen. What may seem like a perfect racetrack is really an opportunity for occasional accidents from running into the drywall!

Drywall repairs for both walls and ceilings are done using the same methods. A good drywall repair will take thought, time, and patience to complete so that the repair is not noticeable.

DIMPLING

Small Holes

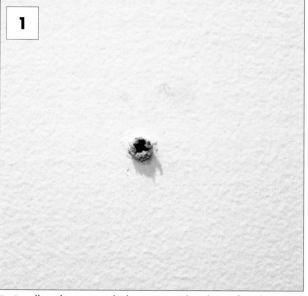

1 Small nail or screw holes require dimpling after the fastener has been removed. This type of repair is the most common when taking pictures down or redecorating a room.

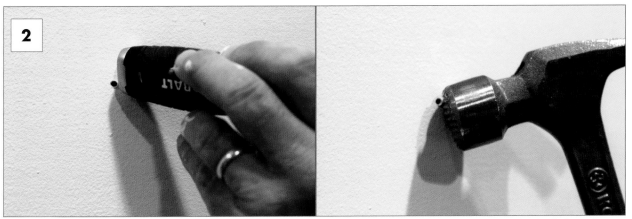

2 Using the metal end of the spackling knife (left) or the edge of the hammer face (right), slightly dimple the hole's edge around the perimeter. When the hole is not dimpled, the hole will create a high spot in the wall.

Medium Holes

Large Holes

1 Medium-size holes created when removing a wall anchor or toggle bolt will require the hole edge to be dimpled in the same way as a small hole. Note: The spackling finish of these screw holes will be covered in the Drywall Finish Repairs section.

1 Large holes created by doorknobs or other damage can be fixed using a simple method with excellent results. Using a straightedge and torpedo level, draw horizontal and vertical lines around, but outside of, the damaged area.

Chapter 2 | Drywall Issues

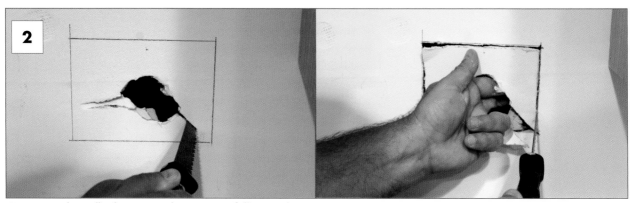

2 Using a drywall jab saw, cut the opening, following the lines drawn to create a straight cut.

3 Cut a piece of wood generally ½ to ¾ inch in thickness and 2 to 3 inches longer than the vertical lines drawn on the drywall.

4 Attach a drywall screw to the center of the wood piece with a cordless drill to hold the wood piece inside the drywall repair cutout.

5 Insert the wood piece into the drywall repair cutout, centered, and install a 1 ⅝-inch drywall screw at one end.

Chapter 2 | Drywall Issues

6 Attach the second 1 ⅝-inch drywall screw to the other end and fasten it tight to the back of the drywall when the screws are tightened. Remove the center screw from the wood piece. Measure the width and height of the drywall repair cutout.

7 Measure and mark a new piece of drywall about ³⁄₁₆ inch shorter in height and length than the drywall repair cutout opening. Use a straightedge to connect the horizontal and vertical marks to create the cut lines. When cutting the drywall, use a drywall jab saw to saw the first, shorter line drawn for the piece size.

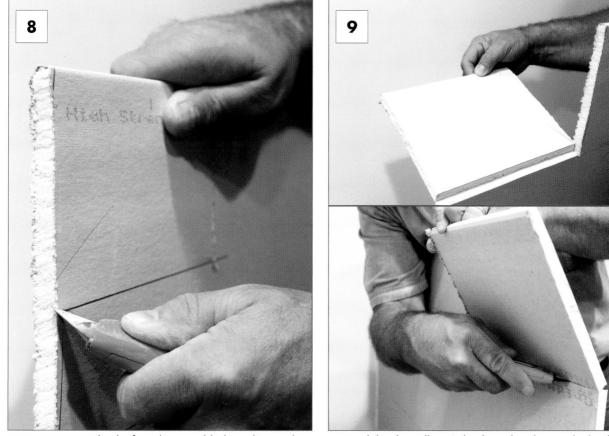

8 Next, use a utility knife with a new blade and score the second, longer line drawn for the piece size.

9 Bend the drywall piece backward and score the back paper to separate the piece from the rest of the sheet.

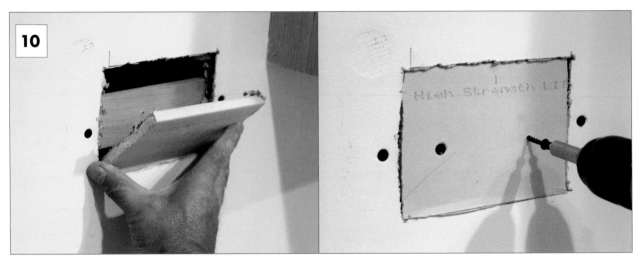

10 Install the repair piece in the drywall repair cutout and secure it to the wood block previously installed in the opening with 1⅝-inch drywall screws. Note: Use the minimum number of screws to attach the repair piece. Caution must be taken not to apply excessive pressure when attaching the repair piece so that the screws holding the wood block in place do not push through the drywall.

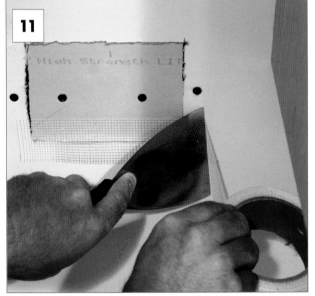

11 Apply self-stick mesh tape along the bottom seam of the repair piece first. Be sure the tape overlaps the vertical cut edges by 1 inch.

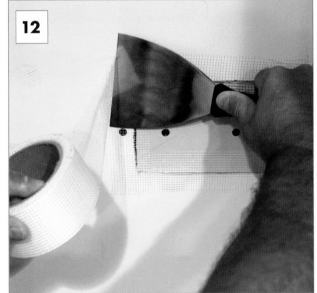

12 Next, apply the mesh tape on each vertical side, even with the bottom piece overlapping at the corners, and extend past the top horizontal cut edge by 1 inch. Lastly, apply the mesh tape to the top seam, overlapping the vertical pieces at the corners but flush with the outer edges of the vertical pieces. Note: Use the 4-inch taping knife to cut the mesh tape. If this is difficult, use the utility knife.

Drywall Repairs before Spackling

DRYWALL FINISH REPAIRS

SKILL LEVEL

- Semiskilled

TOOLS REQUIRED

- #2 Phillips head screwdriver
- Hammer
- Utility knife
- Pole sander
- Hand sander
- 4-, 6-, 8-, and 10-inch spackle knives
- Spackle pan

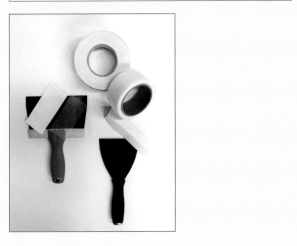

Drywall finish repairs are crucial to fixing damage to drywall walls and ceilings. If this step is not done correctly, the next step—painting—will look even worse, *not better!*

After starting my part-time career in painting when I was a lot younger, it led to working with drywall installation and finishing. The majority of my early drywall finish jobs were through customers who attempted to install their own drywall and had no idea or interest in the finishing aspect.

To start with the correct tools, materials, and techniques is to start any project on the right path. In addition, you have to have enough time to be patient and work through some of the issues that come with working on drywall finish repair projects.

MATERIALS REQUIRED

- Spackle compound
- 220 grit-sand paper
- 2-inch paper tape
- Self-stick mesh tape

Spackling Small, Dimpled Holes

1 To spackle the small holes from wall decorations and pictures that have been dimpled from the drywall repair section is very straightforward. Apply a small amount of spackling to the corner of a 4-inch knife.

2 Place the spackling over the hole and apply pressure to flatten it.

3 Then clean the knife and re-swipe the spackling for a clean first coat. Allow to dry before applying additional coats. Note: Two more spackle coats and light sanding are needed to complete the repair. Remove the sanding dust with a damp sponge.

1 To finish a repair for larger holes in the wall or ceiling, apply a small piece of self-stick mesh tape over the hole. Apply a coat of spackling over the mesh tape, flatten the spackling smooth, and then clean the knife and re-swipe the spackling for a clean first coat. Allow to dry before applying additional coats. Note: Two more spackle coats and light sanding are needed to complete the repair. Remove the sanding dust with a damp sponge.

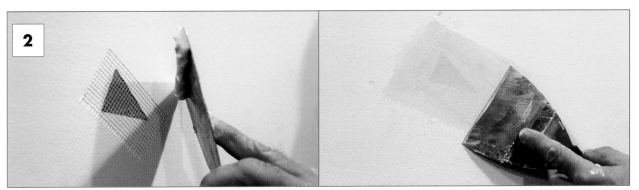

2 To repair a tear in the drywall paper only, cut the loose paper with a utility knife and apply self-stick mesh tape over the cut area. Apply a coat of spackling over the mesh tape, flatten the spackling smooth, and then clean the knife and re-swipe the spackling for a clean first coat. Allow to dry before applying additional coats. Note: Two additional spackle coats and light sanding are needed to complete the repair. Remove the sanding dust with a damp sponge.

Spackling for Large Repairs

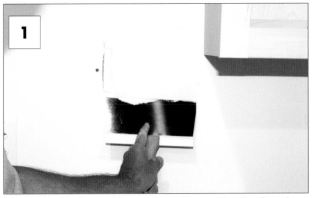

1 Spackle finishing of large drywall repairs will utilize the 8-inch and 10-inch knives and a controllable amount of spackling compound spread over the mesh tape. Use the 8-inch knife in a vertical motion to apply spackle compound. You will use the 8-inch knife because it is slightly wider than the drywall repair piece. Clean the knife and re-swipe the spackling for a clean first coat.

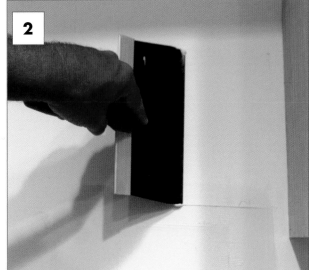

2 After the previous 8-inch coat dries, use an 8-inch knife in a horizontal motion to apply a second coat of spackle compound, and then clean the knife and re-swipe the spackling for a clean second coat. Also be sure to smooth the thick edges.

3 After the second 8-inch coat dries, use a 10-inch knife in a horizontal motion to apply spackling compound for a third coat, and then clean the knife and re-swipe the spackling for a clean third coat. Also be sure to smooth the thick edges. When the spackling coats have dried, use a hand sander with 220-grit sandpaper to provide a sanded smooth surface. Remove the sanding dust with a damp sponge.

Chapter 2 | Drywall Issues

CHAPTER 3

PAINTING BASICS

PAINTING PROJECTS

Painting is a craft that requires detail, patience, planning, and careful execution on the part of the person doing the painting. Painting projects can cover a wide area to a small touch-up spot. The planning and preparation, including obtaining the materials and tools, can seem like it takes the same amount of time regardless of the size of the area.

I have been painting homes since I was fifteen years old. My childhood home's interior was painted by two professional painters. As a five-year-old child, I marveled at what they did and how they did it. I still recall those days, even today, when I am about undertake a painting project!

A good place to start when painting repaired walls and ceilings is to see if you have a can from the last time the room was painted. If the label is legible for pertinent information, then you can match the previous color pretty easily. If you can't find the previous color and are starting from scratch, then the following information will be helpful.

Color matching has now almost become a science of its own. No longer do we simply add a bit more color or white to the can. Everything is done in micro-ounces using a paint-mixing computer. Every paint retail outlet will have plenty of paint color samples on cards to choose from. If you're like me and are challenged by selecting colors, you may have to take the color sample cards home to decide. They are free, so take several to check areas of the room where the sun hits and where it doesn't so there are no surprises when you paint the room.

The key to a successful paint project is the tools that you already have and those that you may need to replace or still need to purchase. There is no substitute for the correct painting tools to accomplish the job just as well as professionals do.

It's important to have a quality large drop cloth or a few smaller ones. Nothing spells disaster more than kicking a new can of paint over on the finished floor surface. Even a small paint spill can feel just as disastrous.

I *do not* recommend plastic drop cloths because they can become extremely slippery on hard, smooth floor finishes. They may, however, be used to cover furniture or other things that are too heavy to move out of the way.

Because prepping the existing painted surfaces is critical to a quality finished paint project, having the basic prep tools and materials in the following list will be a step in the right direction before applying the new paint.

CAUTION

Because paint that was made prior to 1985 may contain lead, it is a good idea to purchase a lead paint test kit at the home-supply center before beginning any paint prep work. Newer paint may be hiding the lead paint underneath!

Lead that is in paint is harmful to small children and females of childbearing ages. Care has to be taken to contain the paint chips, and proper vacuuming and disposal of the chips must be followed according to the local code of your municipality.

Paint prep tools

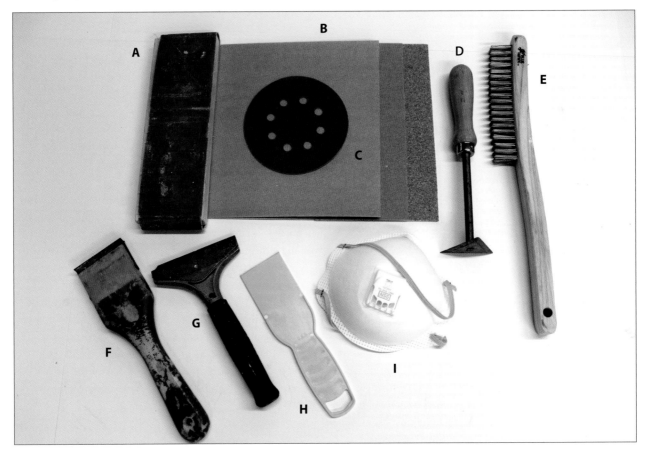

(top, left to right)

    A - sanding block with 80-grit belt sander belt

    B - 80-, 150-, and 220-grit sandpaper

    C - self-stick orbital 150-grit disc

    D - triangle scraping tool

    E - wire brush

(bottom, left to right)

    F - paint scraper with spring blade

    G - paint scraper with razor blade

    H - plastic putty knife

    I - N90 dust mask

The prep tools will help to remove peeled paint and rough high-gloss painted surfaces to accept new primer and finish paint. Sandpaper grit numbers represent the sand grains on the paper: 80 grit is extremely rough, 150 grit is used next, and final sanding will require the 220 grit. The use of power sanding tools requires extreme care so that you don't do too much sanding that distorts or removes the profile of the object being sanded. Caution: Use a quality dust mask or respirator when sanding paint and wood surfaces. Fine dust particles are very easy to inhale and can cause long-term effects to your respiratory system.

Using quality paint brushes is just as important as using quality primer and finish paints. A brush that has seen better days and has a permanent bend in the bristles will not perform like a brush that has been taken care of.

- For water-based latex, use brushes made of synthetic bristles.
- For oil-based paints, use brushes made of natural bristles.

Paintbrush tools

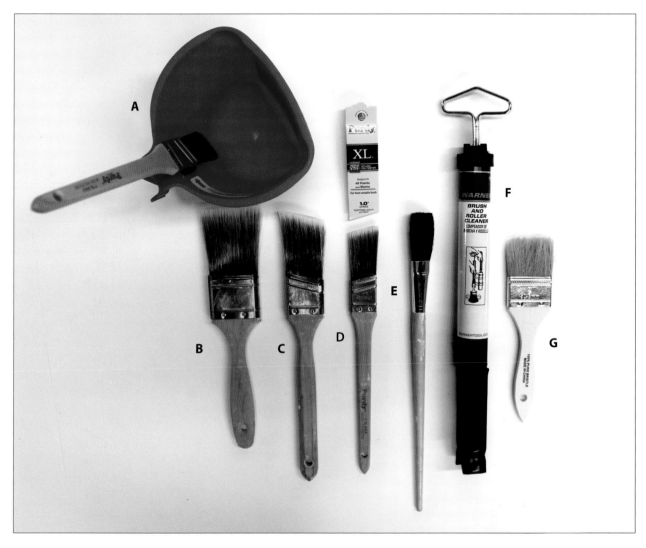

(left to right)
- **A - brush and paint pail**
- **B - 2-inch flat brush**
- **C - 1½-inch tapered sash brush**
- **D - 1-inch tapered sash brush**
- **E - ¾-inch sash brush**
- **F - brush spinner**
- **G - 2-inch chip brush**

This photo shows the type of brushes that are commonly used today to accomplish a high-quality finished project.

Chapter 3 | Painting Basics

Brush Maintenance

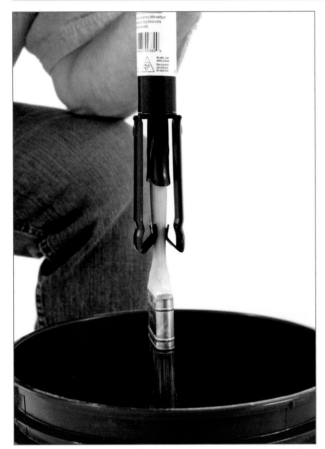

1 The best way to maintain the quality of the bristles of the brush is to thoroughly clean the brush with warm water for latex paints or mineral spirits for oil-based paints. Use a brush spinner and an empty 5-gallon bucket to spin the brush. This opens up the bristles as the brush is being spun and cleans the inside and outside of the brush.

2 Continue to wash and spin the brush until it is free of paint. When the brush is clean, use a quality brush comb to separate the bristles and remove any leftover paint particles between the bristles.

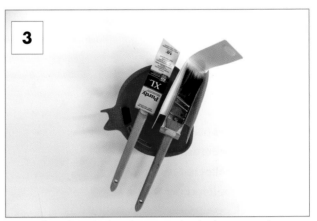

3 Finally, when the brush is completely dry, insert the brush back into the cardboard cover that it came in to keep the bristles straight.

Paint roller tools

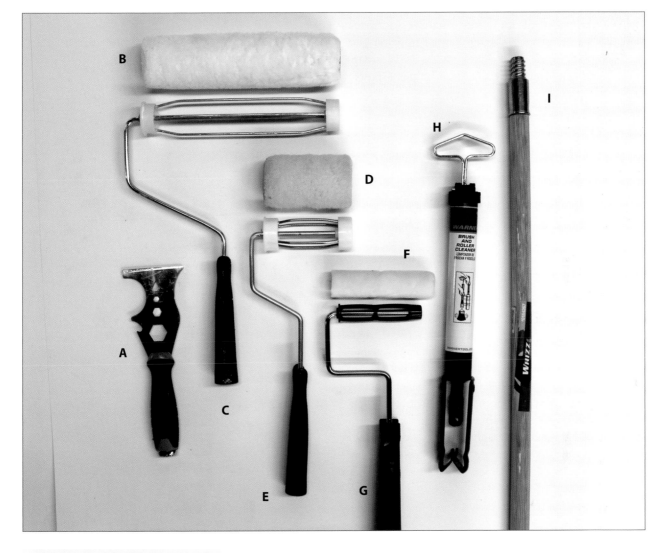

(left to right)

- A - **five-way painter's tool**
- B - **9-inch roller cover**
- C - **9-inch roller handle**
- D - **4-inch roller cover**
- E - **4-inch roller handle**
- F - **6-inch roller cover**
- G - **6-inch roller handle**
- H - **roller spinner**
- I - **4-foot extension pole**

Paint rollers are available in many sizes, materials, and nap thicknesses. Choosing the right one will depend on the project and the desired finish. For most projects, a quality 9-inch-wide roller with a ⅜-inch nap will work very well. For textured walls and ceilings, a ¾-inch nap may be required.

Paint rollers are also produced in different widths and diameters. The 3- and 4-inch-wide rollers are the same diameter as the 9-inch-wide rollers. The 6-inch-wide rollers are smaller in diameter so they can fit in tight places, such as behind the water tank of the toilet.

The photo shows the different rollers and the tools used to achieve a high-quality finished project.

Roller Maintenance

The best way to maintain the quality of a roller cover is to wash it in warm water when using latex paints. If you used the roller cover for oil-based paints, it is best to discard the cover. It will require extensive amounts of mineral spirits to clean.

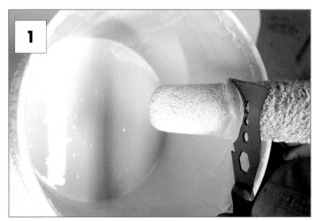

1 A roller has the ability to hold a large amount of paint deep in the nap even when it seems like it is out of paint when rolling on the wall. Use the five-way painter's tool to squeeze the excess paint back into the paint container. Note: If a five-way painter's tool is not available, use the handle end of a paint stir stick. The curved surfaces of the paint-stick handle are made to do the same job. Make sure to rotate the roller and use the tool or paint stir stick around all 360 degrees.

2 During the warm-water wash of the roller cover, place it over the roller spinner and use a 5-gallon bucket to spin the excess paint from the roller cover. Continue to wash and spin until the cover is free of paint. Allow to air-dry standing up on its end.

PRECISION MASKING TAPE

SKILL LEVEL

- Basic

TOOLS REQUIRED

- Utility knife with sharp blades

MATERIALS REQUIRED

- Painters tape of different widths for different applications

Painting finished surfaces can be challenging and time consuming, and a mess can be created if care is not exercised along the way. To avoid some of the pitfalls created by even some of the best painters, masking areas that paint is not desired to be on is the answer.

Just ask any body shop repair technician and they will assure you this is true when they paint a doorjamb of a car with the door off and not a spec of paint can be found on the interior of the car.

Walls are generally painted with rollers first, then the trim is painted by brush second. Where the wall meets the top of the baseboard is not masked, because the top edge of the baseboards is usually thin and can be a challenge for novice painters.

The finished floors where the trim meets it is also another challenge. Since gravity can work against painters and pull the paint down the trim onto the floor as it dries, we spend an enormous amount of time masking the floor to reduce cleanup.

For best results with masking unwanted finished surfaces, use the type of masking paint intended for painters. There are several types available today. Refrain from using the regular masking tape, and don't leave any masking tape on for too long.

MASKING THE WALL FOR PAINTING BASEBOARDS

1 If the wall requires masking at inside corners, we place a piece of painter's masking tape from the inside corner, extending slightly onto the other wall.

2 The second piece of tape for the inside corner overlaps the small piece set previously on that wall.

Chapter 3 | Painting Basics

MASKING THE FLOOR FOR PAINTING BASEBOARDS

1 To mask the bottom of the baseboard or shoe molding, we mask the floor from the inside corner of the trim along the wall. To complete the masking of the floor at the inside corner, we mask the floor along the second wall with the tape overlapping the first piece and continue along the second wall. **Note: Follow the same instructions above for masking outside corners where baseboard or shoe molding meet the floor.**

MASKING THE FLOOR FOR DOORJAMBS AND CASING TRIM

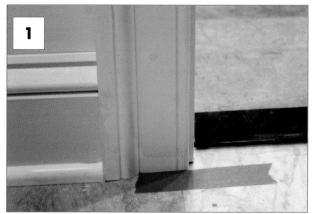

1 Another area needing attention is where the door casing meets the finished floor, especially with the small offset of the reveal between the doorjamb edge and the intricate profiles for casing trim. Start masking the floor at the door casing trim at the floor along the straightest part of the profile and extend into the door opening.

2 Next, apply a piece of tape perpendicular to and over the first piece to include covering the floor at the casing trim reveal of the doorjamb.

3 Apply a piece on the floor along the face of the doorjamb material and overlap the previous piece installed at the casing reveal.

4 Then apply a short piece on the floor that follows the profile of the trim. The more intricate the profile, the more individual short pieces will be required, overlapping the last piece with each additional piece.

5 Apply the long piece of tape along the floor that will go from the last straight profile of the casing trim, and go along the length of the baseboard or shoe molding. Continue masking the floor for the rest of the baseboard or shoe molding until you reach the starting point.

MASKING THE WALLS FOR PAINTING WINDOW AND DOOR TRIM

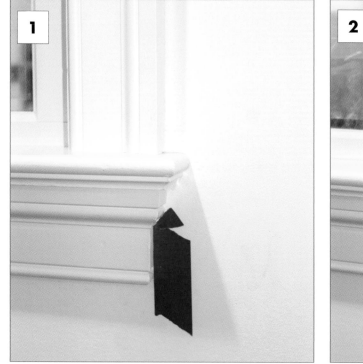

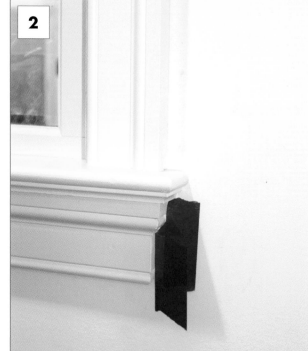

1 First apply painter's tape at the long side of the apron return, including a small piece at the top to start the profile masking.

2 Then apply a small piece of tape over the previous one to continue the next straight profile section.

Chapter 3 | Painting Basics

4 To prevent unwanted paint from getting onto the finished painted wall, apply tape along the straight vertical casing and along the bottom edge of the window apron.

3 Apply a small piece of tape over the previous one along the bottom profile of the trim nosing, then apply a small piece of tape over the previous one and continue masking the top profile of the trim nosing.

Precision Masking Tape

MASKING OF DOOR HINGES

Door hinge leaves attached to the door and doorjamb can create a challenge when painting. Do you take the time to remove the door hinge pins and separate the door from the jamb? Do you then remove each hinge leaf totally? Finally, what happens when you can't get that last screw out to remove the hinge leaf anyway?

An alternative to the above questions is to apply painter's tape precisely, although you will still have to remove the hinge pins to remove the door from the jamb.

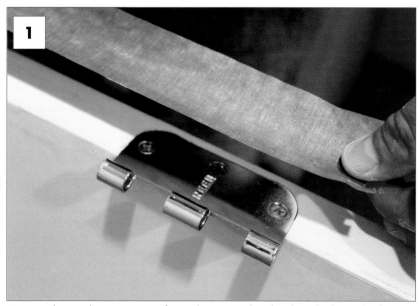

1 Begin by applying a piece of tape longer and wider than the hinge leaf on the door and/or jamb.

2 Using a utility knife with a very sharp blade, score the tape by following the outline of the hinge leaf.

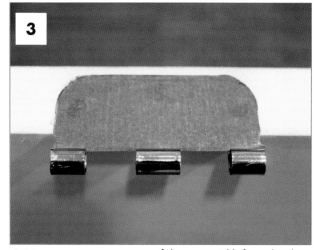

3 Next, remove any excess of the tape width from the door and/or jamb, only covering the entire hinge leaf so it is protected from unwanted paint.

Precision Masking Tape

APPLYING PAINT WITH A BRUSH

SKILL LEVEL

- Basic

TOOLS REQUIRED

- Drop cloth
- Four-way screwdriver
- Brushes
- Paint pail
- Brush comb
- Spinner

MATERIALS REQUIRED

- Primer
- Finish paint
- Paint stir sticks
- Sandpaper
- Tack cloths

When using a brush to apply paint to new bare wood, you need a wood primer product. You can purchase this at your local home-supply center in either latex gallon-sized containers or oil-based quart-sized containers.

Make sure that you select the correct type of primer for either interior or exterior applications. Also, make sure that the primer is the type that requires sanding after drying because this will create the best adhesion quality for the paint.

Open the primer can and use a paint stir stick to thoroughly stir the paint. This mixes the solids and admixtures together for the best priming result. Next, select the width of the brush relative to the area being primed. A narrow brush will require multiple passes of the brush over the surface and thus increase the number of brushstrokes and take more time. Too wide of a brush will allow paint to fall off the brush past the wood edge and onto areas that will require additional cleanup.

1 Apply primer over the face of the new wood to be covered. Be sure that the brush has adequate paint on it, and brush in the direction of the grain of the wood. Cover the entire area of this surface with primer before moving on to other adjacent surfaces.

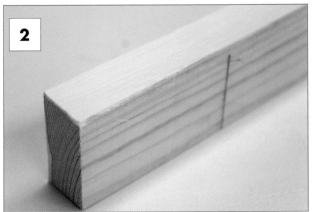

2 Continue to cover other surfaces of the bare wood and use care to keep sharp edges from paint buildup that can run or become unsightly. Cover the entire adjacent surfaces and be sure that excessive paint doesn't build up at the end of the board or on unpainted back surfaces.

Chapter 3 | Painting Basics

3 Allow the primer to dry according to the instructions on the can or longer in high-humidity conditions. Use 150-grit sandpaper to lightly sand the dried primer coat. Be sure to sand in the direction of the wood grain only. **Do not** oversand sharp corners, as this will round them and possibly remove the primer coat.

4 Use a quality tack cloth damp with water to remove any sanding dust on the primer surface. Do not use paper towels. Open the finish paint container and stir the contents with a paint stir stick to mix the solids and admixtures together. Dip the brush into the container and apply the first coat of finish paint over the sanded primer coat. Continue applying finish paint from the brush onto the entire length of the board being painted. Be sure to dip the brush often into the can so that bristles flex to apply the paint, requiring fewer brushstrokes.

5 Be sure to paint all adjacent sides of the board with the brush. You must take care so that the corners do not build up with excessive paint that can run or become unsightly. Note: After the first coat has thoroughly dried and before you apply the second coat of finish paint, sand lightly with 220-grit sandpaper to smooth out any heavy brushstrokes or foreign matter in the first finish coat. Use a quality tack cloth damp with water to remove any sanding dust.

Chapter 3 | Painting Basics

Applying Paint with a Brush

APPLYING PAINT WITH A ROLLER

SKILL LEVEL

- Basic

TOOLS REQUIRED

- Drop cloth
- Four-way screwdriver
- Paint roller handle
- 4-foot extension pole
- Roller covers
- Paint tray
- Paintbrush
- Painter's tape
- Sandpaper
- Dust masks
- Large sponge

MATERIALS REQUIRED

- Primer
- Finish paint

Remove any electrical cover plates that are in the area being painted with the roller. You can cut in around the device with a brush if you choose, but I use the roller to roll around the device, which saves time and eliminates the brushstrokes left behind by the brush.

Using a paint roller to apply paint to ceilings and walls can be a challenge. Too much paint on the roller for ceilings, and you get the equivalent of a bird dropping something on your head. Too much on the wall, and you have uneven paint thicknesses that you'll need to spread to avoid having roller marks.

1 Masking areas to protect them from the splatter of the paint roller should be done before any brush cut-ins or rolling begins. More expensive paints produce less paint splatter when rolling. Open the paint can and stir the contents to mix the solids and admixtures together for the best paint color and adhesion to the painted surface. Paint stir sticks are available in 1-gallon and 5-gallon lengths. Ask your paint supplier for some of each, as they are free, when you pick up your paint order.

2 Pour paint from the paint can into the paint tray, preferably with a liner. The liner will make cleanup so much faster; if cleanup time is limited, you can dispose of the liner after you pour the paint back into the paint can. Pour enough paint into the bottom of the paint tray to fill the bottom area. This will provide enough paint to load the roller and leave ample space at the top of the tray. Dip the cut-in brush into the paint at the bottom of the paint tray for small cut-in areas. Use a paint pail to carry with you for larger cut-in areas. Be sure to swipe the back of the brush over the top of the paint tray or along the side of the paint pail to set the paint in the brush bristles.

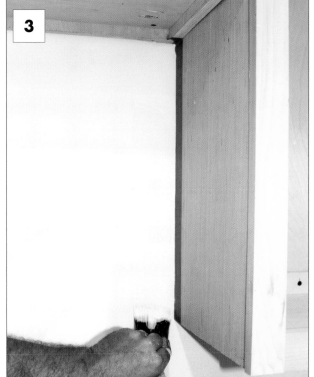

3 Using the brush, cut in all areas where the roller is going to be used so that the paint coat is complete. Rolling over the cut-in brushstrokes with a light amount of paint on the roller cover will give you that professional finish!

4 Attach the 4-foot extension pole to the roller handle. Place the roller with the cover on in the bottom of the paint tray to load paint onto the cover. Roll it around in the paint several times. Raise the roller cover and run it over the top raised ribs of the paint tray to provide an even coat of paint on the roller cover. Apply the paint from the roller cover onto the wall by rolling the roller cover over the wall. Be sure to keep the paint thickness the same each time. As the roller cover requires more paint, place it back in the bottom of the paint tray and repeat the loading of paint into the roller cover. Always overlap the roller onto the last area painted to keep a wet edge.

Applying Paint with a Roller

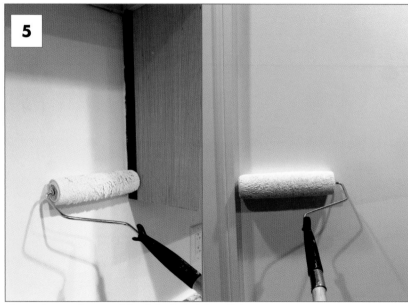

5

CAUTION

Use an appropriate dust mask, N90 or equivalent, when sanding paint between coats. The extremely fine dust particles are easy to inhale into your respiratory system.

✓ TIP

For great primer adhesion of unpainted new drywall, I prefer to let the primer continue to dry overnight. Then, the next morning, lightly sand the primer wall and/or ceiling.

5 For that professional-finish look, lightly roll the cover over the cut-in brush marks to make the brushstrokes disappear!

6

7

6 Sanding primer and/or painted walls and ceilings is preferred between coats to knock down any roller marks or foreign matter that has dried in the fresh coat of paint. Follow the drying time instructions on the paint can, or let the paint dry longer in high-humidity climates.

7 After any sanding of the walls and/or ceilings between coats of paint, use a damp sponge to remove the paint dust caused by sanding. This will reduce the likelihood of the wet roller cover spreading the dust as you paint. The completed and dried project will look as good as any professional's work. All you have to do is follow the instructions and use the tools and methods described here.

Chapter 3 | Painting Basics

CAULK GUN USE

SKILL LEVEL

- Basic

TOOLS REQUIRED

- Utility knife with sharp blades
- 9-ounce caulk gun

MATERIALS REQUIRED

- 9-ounce caulk tube for specified use
- Damp cloth rag

Caulk guns are great tools for applying controlled beads of caulk inside or outside the home. The improvements in the design and performance of today's caulk guns make them superior to those of the 1980s and earlier.

Caulk guns are available in half-shell or open-frame designs. The open-frame design offers much easier loading and unloading of the caulk tube. The trigger mechanism has also been improved; both the ratchet-type trigger and the newer pressure trigger both have good trigger release buttons to stop the flow of caulk. A newer model will have a puncture pin attached to the side of the caulk gun to eliminate needing a long pin to puncture the foil seal inside many caulk tubes. It may also include a cutting blade in the trigger handle to eliminate the need for a utility knife to cut open the end of the tube.

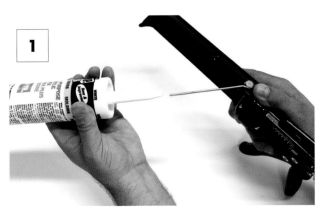

1 Cut a ⅛-inch small opening in the top of the caulk tube with a utility knife or the cutting blade that came with your caulk gun. Use the long pin attached to the side of the caulk gun to poke a hole in the foil seal of the tube

2 Load the tube in the caulk gun and squeeze the trigger to apply caulk to the required area.

3 Move along the area at a steady pace and squeeze the trigger so the caulk flows out of the tube evenly. Push the release button on the back of the caulk gun to stop the flow of caulk. For latex or latex with silicone caulk, use your fingertip to smooth the caulk bead from the caulk gun. Clean the excess off of your finger with the damp cloth rag. When finished caulking, insert a small nail into the ⅛-inch opening at the end of the tube. Wrap the outside of the tube with tape to prevent the caulk at the end of the tube from drying out.

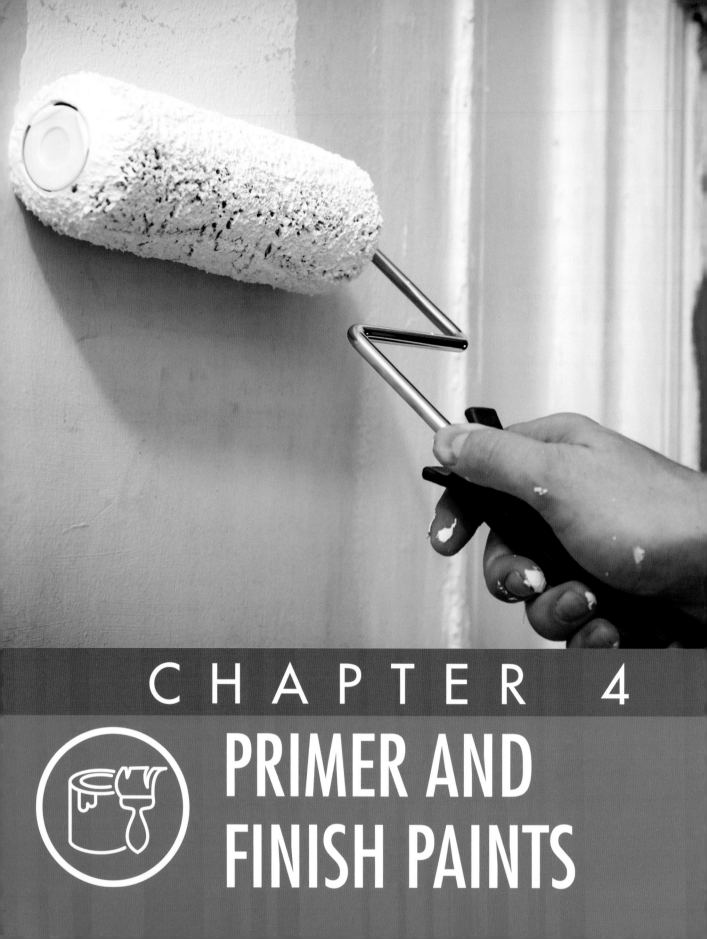

CHAPTER 4

PRIMER AND FINISH PAINTS

CALCULATING GALLONS OF PRIMER AND FINISH PAINTS

Calculate the number of gallons needed for one coat of latex primer for new drywall by adding up the square area of the wall and ceiling surfaces. Large window and door areas can be deducted from the total. Standard doors should not be deducted. Divide the total area by 250 square feet per gallon, and this should be adequate for one coat.

A 12 x 12-foot room with 8-foot-high walls equals 384 square feet for the walls and 144 square feet for the ceiling; this equals 576 square feet to be covered without any deductions for windows and doors. Three 1-gallon cans of primer would be required.

If the ceiling will be a different finish color than the rest of the walls, divide the ceiling area by 300 square feet per gallon to find out how much finish paint you will need for one coat. If using a flat white ceiling color, then one coat should work well over the white primer coat. If the ceiling color is not white, then add approximately another 50 percent to the first coat quantity for the second coat. The 12 x 12-foot ceiling would require ¾ gallon for two coats.

The finish-paint quantity for the walls will be the entire area of all wall surfaces divided by 300 square feet per gallon. Add approximately another 50 percent to the first finish-coat quantity for the second coat. The four 12 x 12 x 8-foot high walls, without window and door deductions, would require 2 gallons for two coats.

To determine if a previously painted surface is water-based or oil-based paint is straightforward. Pour denatured alcohol on a rag. Rub the rag vigorously over the painted surface. If the paint color rubs off onto the rag, it is a water-based paint.

Make sure all primers and paints are shaken well by the paint department before you head home. It is standard

practice for customers to check and approve mixed colors before paying for them. A computer formula is printed for the paint that is tinted, but mistakes can happen. **Tinted paint is usually not refundable for choosing the wrong color!**

After deciding how many gallons of each type and color of paint that you'll need, let's explore the many sheens and bases to find out which are best suited for your project. Caution: Any existing paint in the building that exists prior to 1985 is suspect of containing lead. This can be harmful to small children and females of child bearing ages. Obtain a lead test kit from the local Home Center to be sure.

✓ TIP

When new latex paint must be painted over a previous oil-based paint, the use of a quality latex primer coat is required first. Allow the primer coat to dry thoroughly. Lightly sand the surface between coats and remove the dust with a damp sponge.

Drywall primer/sealer is a water-based paint with excellent sealing qualities for bare drywall and outstanding adhesion to drywall paper and spackling compound. Water-based latex interior paints are intended to be used over previous coats of water-based latex paints and primer for drywall. This paint is *not* intended to be used over oil-based finish paints because it will create a low adhesion quality between the new water-based latex paint and previous oil-based paint. The new latex will eventually shed itself from the oil-based paint in large, easy-to-pull-off sections.

Water-based exterior enamel paints are intended to be painted over previous coats of water-based paints and over new wood-sanding primers. This paint is not intended to be painted over oil-based finish paints without first using a primer that is capable of being sanded. This will create a high adhesion quality for the new coat of water-based latex enamel paint.

Oil-based enamel paints are intended to be painted over previously oil based painted surfaces and over new wood sanding primers. These include interior and exterior locations.

Paint sheens are available in flat, eggshell, satin, semigloss, and gloss.

- **Flat finish** is the most forgiving on walls and ceilings for touch-ups. That annoying spot behind the front door where the doorknob hits the wall and creates a divot in the drywall? This 2–inch-diameter divot can be spackled, sanded, primed, and painted in two coats without having to paint the entire wall.

- **Eggshell finish** provides a slight sheen for light reflection and a smoother wall surface for cleaning fingerprints left behind by little hands! Touch-up spots require more attention to blending the eggshell-finish paint with the surrounding area of existing wall or ceiling paint.

- **Satin finish** provides a slightly higher sheen for light reflection and is easier to clean. Touch-up spots require greater attention; it's very difficult to blend satin-finish paint, so you'll need to repaint the entire wall or ceiling.

- **Semigloss** and gloss finishes are meant for trim only. They are the easiest to clean. Touching up any damaged wood will require you to repaint the entire piece of wood to blend this sheen with the remaining trim.

Calculating Gallons of Primer and Finish Paints

APPLYING STAIN-BLOCKING PRIMERS

SKILL LEVEL

- Basic

TOOLS REQUIRED

- Paint brush
- Stir stick

MATERIALS REQUIRED

- Alcohol
- Oil- or water-based stain-blocking primer

When dealing with wood and other materials that can absorb moisture for periods of time, the material can be permanently stained. No matter how many coats of the best latex or oil-based paint you use, the stain will eventually work its way to the surface. This applies to all interior and exterior painted surfaces.

New wood that contains knots or very dark streaks in the wood grain that can also create problems when painting. The only wood knots that do not require our attention are those on finish woods that you are going to stain or apply with a clear coat.

✓ TIP

To clean brushes after using oil-based primer, use mineral spirits; for water-based primer, use water. It is best to discard brushes used with alcohol-based primer.

1 Open the can and use a paint stir stick to thoroughly mix the solids and admixtures. This will create the highest-quality primer coat. Lay the wood piece on a steady surface and apply the stain-blocking primer over the wood knots, wood-grain discolorations, or water stains. Allow the stain-blocking primer to fully dry according to the instructions on the can or longer if high-humidity conditions exist.

2 After the primer coat has dried, sand the piece with 150-grit sandpaper to smooth any irregularities. Wipe with a damp tack cloth prior to applying the finish coat.

Chapter 4 | Primer and Finish Paints

APPLYING FINISH PAINT TO WALLS AND CEILINGS

Maintain the finish paint prep area away for the room or area from the primer coat to protect areas from unwanted paint splatter and avoid unnecessary cleanup. Apply finish paint with a 9-inch roller with a ⅜-inch nap finish. Finish paints are designed to have more solids and admixtures and adhere to the freshly dried primer coat underneath.

Ceiling

A ceiling that will be a different color than the walls requires special attention. Apply the ceiling paint with a 1½-inch tapered paintbrush along the ceiling edges where the ceiling meets the walls. By carefully painting along the ceiling surface only, you won't need to mask the wall with painter's tape. Use the brush to push the paint into the corners.

Apply ceiling paint using a 9-inch roller with a ⅜-inch nap finish. Always roll in the shortest direction of the ceiling. Apply a liberal amount of paint to the center of the 9-inch roller path and roll the paint outward until you cover the desired length or you reach a wall.

Overlap each 9-inch roller pass by 1 inch to maintain a wet paint edge. Reduce paint buildup on the edges by rerolling edges with the roller as it runs out of paint before reloading paint onto the roller in the tray.

Allow the ceiling paint ample time to dry according to the paint can label. Allow more time, if needed, due to temperature and/or humidity differences.

Lightly sand the ceiling paint areas between the first and second coats for the smoothest finish coat possible. Lightly clean the sanded areas using a damp sponge for better adhesion of the second coat of ceiling paint.

Walls

Walls that will be a different color than the ceiling require special attention. After you've applied the necessary number of ceiling coats, and the ceiling is completely dry, apply the wall paint to the top edge of all walls with a 1½-inch tapered paintbrush. By carefully painting along the top wall edge only, you won't need to mask the ceiling with painter's tape. Use the brush to push the paint into the corners.

Next, brush the vertical inside wall corners and any other places where either a 4-inch or 9-inch roller won't fit.

Lastly, brush paint along the wall at the top of baseboards and along all of the door and window trim. Always start at the top of the wall and work your way to the bottom. If any paint drips, then just brush that paint smooth as you work your way downward.

Apply wall paint using a 9-inch roller with a ⅜-inch nap finish. Apply a liberal amount of paint to the center of the 9-inch roller path and roll the paint until you cover the desired length.

Overlap each 9-inch roller pass by 1 inch to maintain a wet paint edge. Reduce paint buildup on the edges by rerolling the edges with the roller as it runs out of paint before reloading paint onto the roller in the tray.

Allow the wall paint ample time to dry according to the paint can label. Allow more time, if needed, due to temperature and/or humidity differences.

Lightly sand the wall paint areas between the first and second coats for the smoothest finish coat possible. Lightly clean sanded areas using a damp sponge for better adhesion of the second coat of wall paint.

PAINTING STAINED CABINETS AND TRIM

SKILL LEVEL

- **Basic**

TOOLS REQUIRED

- **4-way screwdriver**
- **N90 dust masks**
- **Paintbrush**
- **Paint stir stick**

MATERIALS REQUIRED

- **Stain-blocking primer**
- **Sandpaper**
- **Finish paint**
- **Tack cloths**

Interior finish styles can change often and even be mixed between rooms and within the same room. Wood surfaces originally finished in stain and clear coat can be changed to a finished painted surface fairly easily.

✓ TIP

You must use an N90 dust mask so that fine dust particles do not enter your respiratory system. After sanding the clear coat finish, remove the dust by using a lint-free cloth (tack cloth). Slightly dampen the cloth so it picks up the dust instead of just moving the dust around.

1 To begin, remove the hardware from the stained item being painted and set aside for later reuse. I also recommend that you address any nicks, holes, or other blemishes of the original stained wood during this phase. Use wood filler, sandpaper, or stain-blocking primer to cover wood knots.

2 The original clear coat over the stain was used to seal the wood and prevent water or moisture from penetrating the surface. You have to "dull" or scuff the clear coat with 180 or 220 fine-grit sandpaper so that the wood will accept the primer/stain-blocking coat.

Chapter 4 | Primer and Finish Paints

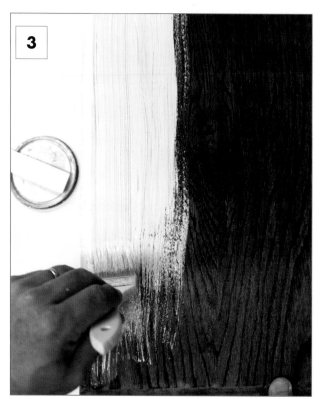

3 Open the can of primer/stain-blocking paint and use a paint stir stick to mix the solids of the paint evenly so that they do not sit on the bottom of the can. The primer can either be oil based or water based; choose based on the environment you will be working in and your cleanup preferences. Oil-based primer requires chemical thinners and cleaners, while you need only water for water-based primer. Use a quality brush of a size appropriate to the coverage area: a 1½-inch tapered brushed for smaller areas, and a 2- to 3-inch straight brush for wider areas. Begin at one corner and apply the primer along the entire length of the surface in the direction of the wood grain. Smooth the primer as you go to reduce brush marks, and keep a wet paint edge as you progress across the surface.

✓ *TIP*

I do not recommend applying a second coat of primer/stain blocker unless an area didn't receive an appropriate coat or a blemish from a wood knot is bleeding through the primer.

✓ *TIP*

Use synthetic brushes with water-based primers and natural brushes with oil-based brushes. Do not use synthetic brushes with oil-based primers.

4 After the primer/stain-blocking coat has dried, preferably at least eight hours, sand the surface to remove any unwanted debris and heavy brush marks in the finish. Starting the first coat of the finish paint color is the same process as with the primer/stain-blocking coat. The correct brush is required for the type of paint you are using, either water-based or oil-based, and the brush should be an appropriate width for the area you are painting.

✓ *TIP*

For the best finish-paint adhesion, use an oil-based primer/stain-blocking coat with either water- or oil-based finish paints.

I recommend allowing the first coat to dry for at least eight hours and then sanding lightly with 220-grit sandpaper and a tack cloth dampened with water to remove the dust. Follow with a second (and third, if needed) coat with light sanding between those coats. Note: You must use an N90 dust mask so that fine dust particles do *not* enter your respiratory system.

Finish paint sheens can be eggshell, satin, semigloss, and gloss. The higher the sheen, the more noticeable defects will be in your finished painted cabinets or trim, but it will be easier to clean.

Chapter 4 | Primer and Finish Paints

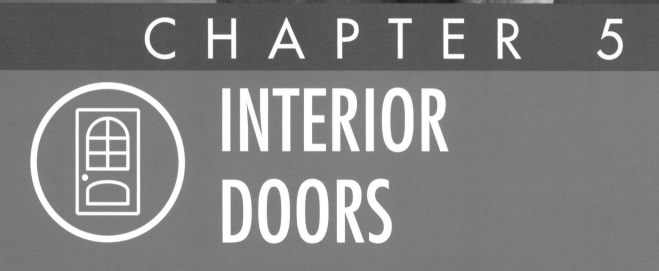

CHAPTER 5

INTERIOR DOORS

INTERIOR DOORSTOPS

SKILL LEVEL

- Basic

TOOLS REQUIRED

- Pencil
- Tape measure
- Hammer
- Small punch or nail
- Cordless drill
- Small twist drill bit
- Adjustable wrench

MATERIALS REQUIRED

- Baseboard-mounted or hinge pin doorstop

Doorstops are used for in-swing interior and exterior doors to prevent damaging the wall behind the door with the doorknob, which often occurs when someone is in a hurry and flings the door wide open. It also can occur on windy days with the front and back doors.

Doorstops are available in different styles, materials, and finishes. The two most commonly used types of doorstops are baseboard mounted and hinge pin. The baseboard-mounted style is the oldest and most widely used because doors were designed to open against a wall surface. These doorstops have become challenging to install in newer-style homes because of the desirable open floor plans.

BASEBOARD MOUNTED

Position the doorstop along the baseboard to provide the maximum door opening and so that the inside doorknob will not strike the finished wall surface. A baseboard-mounted doorstop has a screw-style threadpost that threads itself into the wooden baseboard. A predrilled hole smaller than the screw's diameter is beneficial for ease of installing.

1 To accomplish this, we use a portable drill with a small twist drill bit to produce the hole.

2 If a small twist bit isn't available, you can insert a small finish nail into the drill chuck to produce the hole. Start turning the threaded end of the baseboard-mounted doorstop into the pilot hole and tighten with an adjustable wrench. Take care not to scratch the finished metal surface with the wrench. When the baseboard-mounted doorstop is tight, the wide flange base will fit snugly against the flat baseboard surface.

HINGE PIN

A hinge pin doorstop gives the flexibility to stop a door when a wall does not extend beyond the edge of the door. Another situation is when the wall extends past the path of the door but furniture or other obstructions prohibit the use of a baseboard-mounted stop. Hinge pin doorstops require the use of two stops: one mounted at the top hinge pin and the second at the bottom hinge pin. This is done to provide the doorstop with maximum strength.

1 Begin by removing the top hinge pin with a flat-end punch or nail.

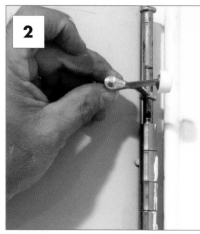

2 Install the hinge pin through the hole in the hinge stop. The hinge stop has an adjustable threaded stem with a rubber stop on the end. The other side is a fixed length with a rubber stop on the end.

3 Reinstall the hinge pin back into the hinge assembly and make sure that the head of the pin comes in contact with the hinge stop. Adjust the threaded stem to provide for the maximum door swing without the inside knob damaging the finished wall surface. Remove the bottom hinge pin and install the hinge stop in the same manner as the top hinge stop.

✓ TIP

Make sure that the bottom hinge stop is adjusted equally to the top hinge stop. This provides maximum strength and protection when someone comes flying into the room! The advantage of the hinge pin stop is that it can rotate with the door, providing the maximum benefit of stopping a door that has been swung open very fast.

Chapter 5 | Interior Doors

INTERIOR DOOR LOCKSETS

Interior door locksets come in several types, styles, and finishes. To understand which type you need, we must understand the purpose of each.

Interior door locksets will have a 2⅛-inch diameter bore hole for the lockset and have a 2⅜-inch backset distance from the edge of the door to the center of the hole.

Passage locksets are the simplest and least expensive type. They simply allow the door to be latched in the closed position and opened with the twist of the knob. This type is used on closet and basement doors. When installing, it's preferable to have the exposed mounting screws in the closet or facing the basement side of the doorway.

Privacy locksets are used to provide privacy or restricted access into a room, such as bedrooms, bathrooms, and basements. Even though a basement door can have a passage lock, a privacy lock can add additional security to the house entrance from a basement.

The exposed mounting screws will always be on the side of the door on which the knob lock is located. The most common lock is a center-twist tab, and there are also twist-and-push and push-button styles.

To open a locked privacy lockset, you'll need a pin key, which is included with the lock and can be stored above the door on the trim casing. If the pin key is missing, use a tiny screwdriver, long nail, or other similar instrument to unlock the door through the pin-sized hole on the faceplate or the doorknob. This is helpful to know! When one of my grandsons was two, he locked himself in his room. His mother called me while his father went out to buy another lock—but in a few minutes I had the door unlocked, and my grandson was running around the house again!

Finishes for interior locksets can be bright brass, bronze, and satin nickel along with a few other finishes. The lockset finish should match the finish of the hinge leaves. If the hinge leaves are painted, you can use a lockset in any of the available finishes.

The most common knob styles are Bell and Plymouth. Bell knobs are long, slender, and tapered with flat ends. Plymouth knobs are shallow with round ends. Also, since the passing of the Americans with Disability Act (ADA), ADA-compliant locksets have been made with paddle-style push handles to eliminate the requirement of having to grip a round knob to open a door.

Another key part of the correct operation of an interior lockset is the strike plate. The strike plate is mounted to the slam side of the doorjamb in a routed recess to make it flush with the wood jamb when installed with the two wood screws. The strike plate has a bent tab in the backset opening. This tab is adjustable by slightly bending it toward the straight side of the backset opening. This will lessen the gap and door movement to reduce rattling when the door is latched in the closed position.

Adjustable strike plate tab.

REPLACING INTERIOR LOCKSETS

SKILL LEVEL

- Basic

TOOLS REQUIRED

- #2 Phillips head screwdriver

MATERIALS REQUIRED

- Correct lockset replacement

Most interior locksets can be installed and replaced while the door is attached to the hinges. Sometimes, it is an advantage to remove the door from the jamb by taking out the hinge pins and then placing the door in a door jack to secure the door. A door jack can be beneficial for holding a door, especially an older, heavier door, along its long edge. The door jack can be made of scrap materials. The function of the jack allows the thin base to flex from the door's weight, and the vertical sides of the triangular pieces pinch the door sides to secure it.

Door jacks can easily be made of scrap material.

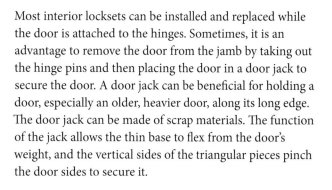

1 To replace an interior lockset, locate the screws that hold the lockset halves together. Use a #2 Phillips-head screwdriver to loosen and remove the screws. Using both hands, remove both halves of the lockset from the door. One half will have a pin that goes through the backset. Loosen and remove the two screws that secure the backset in the door edge recess pocket. Remove the two screws that secure the strike plate on the slam side of the doorjamb.

Chapter 5 | Interior Doors

2

2 Unpack the new lockset and install the universal backset that works with both interior and exterior doors. Secure the backset with the two supplied Phillips screws into the door edge recess.

3

3 Unpack the new doorknob set and install the knob half, with the pin engaging in the backset.

4

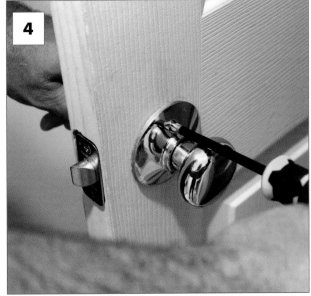

4 Install the other knob half with the screw holes and engage the knob in the pin protruding through the backset. Install the two long Phillips screws and tighten with a screwdriver.

5

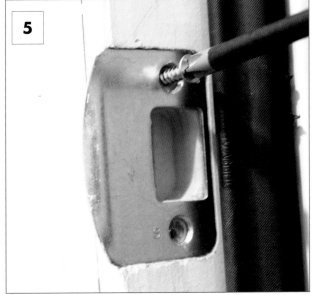

5 Install the new strike plate on the slam side of the doorjamb with one short Phillips screw. Check the alignment and latching of the new lockset. If the new strike plate requires adjustment, complete the adjustment before installing the final Phillips screw.

REPLACING OLDER DOOR LOCKSETS

Older locksets for interior and exterior doors function the same way as the newer ones. However, the installation and removal of these locksets is quite different.

SKILL LEVEL

- **Basic**

TOOLS REQUIRED

- **Small straight screwdriver**
- **Straight screwdriver**
- **# 2 Phillips-head screwdriver**

MATERIALS REQUIRED

- **New-style lockset**

1 Remove an older-style lockset by locating the rectangular locking tab on the inside knob shaft. Use a small straight screwdriver and push the locking tab inward while pulling on the inside doorknob.

2 Locate the slot along the outside edge of the lock escutcheon plate, place the small screwdriver's tip in the slot, and pry the escutcheon plate loose and remove it.

3 Unscrew the two round-head back plate screws and remove the lockset from the bore hole in the door.

4 Unscrew the two flat-head backset screws from the door edge and remove the backset from the door. To install an old lockset, reverse the directions above. Unpack the new lockset and follow the installation instructions. Observe the details of the existing routed recess areas for the backset plate and the strike plate. Some locksets have interchangeable mounting plates for the backset to match square or round corners. Match the plate corner details or chisel round corners square for square-style backset mounting plates.

Chapter 5 | Interior Doors

INTERIOR DOOR PREP AND PAINT

SKILL LEVEL

- **Basic**

TOOLS REQUIRED

- **Phillips-head screwdriver**
- **Drop cloth**
- **Sponge**
- **Paint tray**
- **3- or 4-inch roller handle**
- **⅜-inch roller cover**
- **2-inch paintbrush**

MATERIALS REQUIRED

- **Finish paint**
- **220-grit sandpaper**

Most people, including myself, use a roller to paint walls and ceilings and a brush to paint trim, window sashes, and doors. Imagine my surprise one morning at 6:00 a.m. when I found my painter rolling paint onto interior six-panel raised doors! I said to him, "Rollers are for walls and ceilings. What are you doing?" His reply was, "I always paint doors with a roller first and then use the brush to smooth out the nap from the roller. I paint doors better and faster than anyone else!"

From that day on, so did I. I also use a roller to prepaint flat pieces of wood on sawhorses and then use a brush to smooth out the nap from the roller. That day, it was proven that you can teach an old dog a new trick!

1 To begin, remove any hardware from the door and put it in a safe place. In these photos, we are painting a pocket door, which will remain in place while we paint both sides. Note: If swinging doors can be left in place to paint, both sides can be painted at the same time. See the Precision Masking Tape section (page 31) for how to mask the hinge leaves.

2 Sand any small areas of the door that have damage or marks with 220-grit sandpaper. Use a damp sponge to remove any sanding dust.

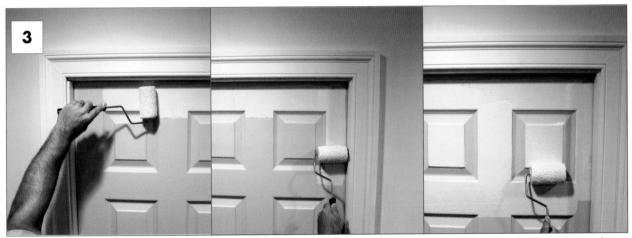

3 Pour the finish paint into a paint tray and use either a 3-inch or 4-inch roller with a ⅜-inch nap to load paint onto the roller. Begin at the top of the door and roll paint onto the flat areas of the door, working your way downward. Note: Roll enough paint onto the door so that it will remain wet and you can use the brush to smooth out the nap from the roller.

4 Brush over the previously rolled flat areas of the door while the paint is still wet to smooth out the nap from the roller.

5 Dip the 2-inch brush into the paint tray to load the brush with paint. Brush the smaller detail areas of the door. Allow the first coat to dry on one side while you repeat the process for the other side of the door. After you've painted the second side of the standing door, begin the second finish coat of the first side using the roller and brush methods. When the second coat is dry on both sides, you too will have painted an interior door in a fast and professional way!

Chapter 5 | Interior Doors

STRIPPED SCREW REPAIRS

SKILL LEVEL

- **Basic**

TOOLS REQUIRED

- **Utility knife with new sharp blades**
- **4-way screwdriver**
- **Door jack**

MATERIAL REQUIRED

- **¼-inch lauan plywood**
- **Wood glue**

Screws that secure hardware items and become loose from being stripped are very problematic. In my career I have come across this issue with many different hinges, from doors and cabinets to just about everything that is wood and gets attached with a screw.

Imagine a door that keeps closing hard because it strikes the doorjamb. This happens on older solid wood doors due to their weight and size and the pressure on the screw heads securing the hinge leaves.

This same condition makes it hard to open a door that is fully closed, because the door drags on the jamb and doesn't have that nickel thickness (⅛–³⁄₁₆ inch) of clearance that doors need for proper operation.

The fix for this condition has been used widely by building professionals with great success and requires very little time and materials. The use of a door jack (see page 49) can help steady the door and provide ample support to fix screw holes that are stripped.

1 Using a utility knife and a ¼-inch-thick scrap piece of plywood that is several inches long, score the plywood lengthwise into pieces approximately ¼ inch wide. Separate the pieces by breaking them apart with your hand, and place yellow wood glue in the hole that is stripped.

Chapter 5 | Interior Doors

2 Place the ¼-inch-wide pieces of plywood in the hole one at a time until the last strip is installed snugly in the hole.

3 After the glue has dried in the hole with the plywood strips installed (roughly 20 minutes), break the strips off one at a time. Use the utility knife to cut any plywood strips that are broken above the recessed area for the hinge.

4 Insert the screw being used in the center of the filled hole, and use a hand screwdriver to start the screw, turning it in a clockwise direction while applying downward pressure. When completed, the stripped screw hole repair will have the same holding power that the remaining unstripped screws have to hold the hinge leaf tight and keep the heavy solid wood door from hitting the door jamb.

Chapter 5 | Interior Doors

Stripped Screw Repairs

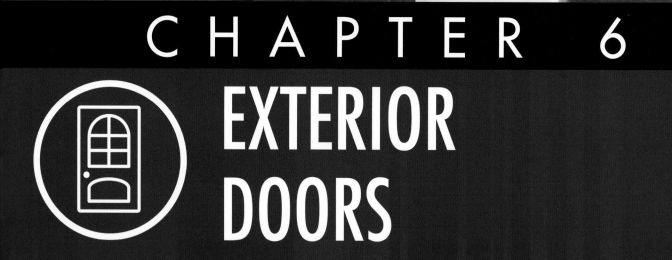

CHAPTER 6

EXTERIOR
DOORS

EXTERIOR DOOR LOCKSETS

Exterior locksets are used more than the interior locksets. Everyone usually goes through the same exterior door to enter and exit the home. Every day, a key is inserted into the lockset at least as many times in a day as there are key holders in the home.

Exterior door locksets come in several types, styles, and finishes. They all have a 2⅛-inch diameter bore hole for the lockset and a 2¾-inch backset distance from the edge of the door to the center of the hole.

Older manufactured backsets are made specifically for

exterior doors. Newer manufactured backsets are universal in design by accommodating interior and exterior locksets in the same part.

Keyed locksets are installed in a similar way to interior locksets except for the keyed knob. This knob must be installed so that the open end of the keyhole slot is facing downward. This will ensure that the tumblers are in the correct position for the key to operate and unlock the knob every time. If it is installed with the open end facing upward, the tumblers can drop down and not allow the key to be inserted completely.

This very scenario happened on a front door we had ready for a spring open house. The front doorknob was installed with the open end of the slot facing upward. The tumblers in the lock would not engage the cut key,

and we had to scramble like mad to get the door to unlock with the key. I immediately found a screwdriver to reverse the key lock knob of the lockset.

Finishes for exterior locksets can be bright brass, bronze, and satin nickel, along with a few other types. The lockset finish should match the hinge leaf finishes. If the hinge leaves are painted, the finish of the lockset can be any of the finishes listed.

Knob styles usually are Bell or Plymouth styles. The Bell shape is long, slender, and tapered with round ends. The Plymouth shape has shallow knobs with round ends. Also, since the passing of the Americans with Disability Act (ADA), locksets are available with paddle arms to eliminate the requirement of gripping a round-style knob to open a door.

Another key part to the correct operation of an exterior lockset is the strike plate. The strike plate is mounted to the slam side of the doorjamb in a routed recess to make it flush with the wood jamb when installed with the two wood screws. The strike plate has a bent tab in the backset opening (see page 48). This tab is adjustable by slightly bending it toward the straight side of the backset opening. This will lessen the gap and door movement to reduce rattling when the door is latched in the closed position.

A door jack can be beneficial to holding a door, especially a heavy exterior door, along its long edge for multiple tasks on the door. The door jack can be made of scrap materials (see page 49). The function of the jack allows the thin base to flex from the door weight, and the vertical sides of the triangular pieces pinch the door sides to secure it.

Most exterior locksets can be installed and replaced while the door is attached to the hinges. Sometimes it helps to remove the door from the jamb by taking out the hinge pins and placing the door in a door jack to secure the door for multiple tasks to be performed on it.

SKILL LEVEL

- Basic

TOOLS REQUIRED

- #2 Phillips head screwdriver

MATERIALS REQUIRED

- New exterior lockset

1 To replace an exterior lockset, locate the screws that hold the lockset halves together. Using a #2 Phillips screwdriver, loosen and remove the screws. Using both hands, remove both halves of the lockset from the door. The one half will have a pin that goes through the backset.

2 Loosen and remove the two screws securing the backset in the door edge recess pocket.

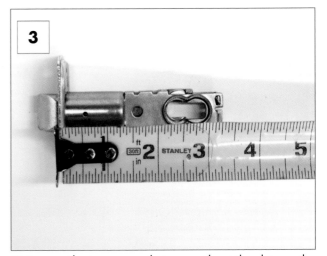

3 Remove the two screws that secure the strike plate on the slam side of the doorjamb (see Step 5 on page 50), then unpack the new lockset and install the universal backset that works with both interior and exterior doors.

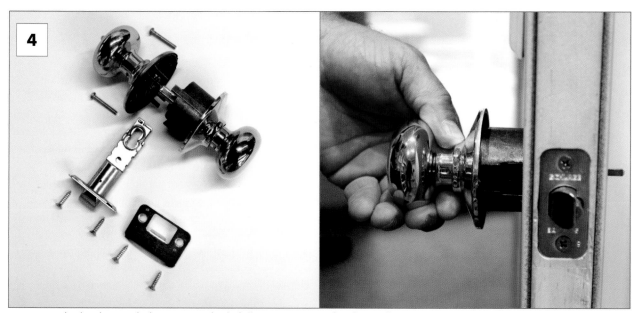

4 Secure the backset with the two supplied Phillips screws into the door edge recess (see Step 2 on page 50). Unpack the new doorknob set and install the key half with the pin engaging in the backset.

5 Install the inside knob half with the screw holes and engage the knob in the pin protruding through the backset. Install the two long Phillips screws and tighten with a hand screwdriver. Install the new strike plate on the slam side of the doorjamb with one short Phillips screw. Check the alignment and latching of the new lockset. If the new strike plate requires adjustment, complete the adjustment before installing the final Phillips screw.

Chapter 6 | Exterior Doors

DOOR SECURITY

SKILL LEVEL

- Semiskilled

TOOLS REQUIRED

- Drill
- Appropriate twist drill bit
- #1 Phillips bit
- Tape measure
- Pencil

MATERIALS REQUIRED

- Interior security lock desired
- Storm door keyed lock if needed

Securing exterior doors today is extremely important for safety and peace of mind whether you are at home, at work, or traveling away for periods of time. Nothing deters someone from entering your residence more than a locked and secured door. I have used these types of door security methods in my own home for the past 35 years.

Exterior locksets covered previously in this chapter are made to withstand anti-picks and are very strong when installed correctly. Of course, a locked and secured door can be battered open by extreme force when the wood jamb splits or the door splits at the lockset, but these are not normal cases.

There are several types of door security latches available to make sure that even if the door lock is able to be unlocked, the door itself can remain closed or have restricted openings by the use of these interior security measures.

The first type of exterior door security is the surface bolt mechanism on the actual door surface, and the matching part is the mortise strike plate. This hardware can be mounted vertically or horizontally and is very effective. However, when the slide bolt is opened, it will not restrict the door from opening completely.

SURFACE BOLT INSTALLATION

1 Locate the desired height of the surface bolt above the exterior lockset, approximately 60 inches above the floor.

2 Locate the holes, using the surface bolt as a template. Drill one $5/64$-inch hole, fasten the surface bolt to the inside surface of the exterior door, and level the bolt.

3. Slide the surface bolt open so it extends past the door edge. Using the rectangular strike plate as a template, locate the two holes, drill with a $5/64$-inch drill, and attach the strike plate with the two screws provided.

4. On the door jamb, position the keep plate where the surface bolt aligns, locate the two holes, drill two $5/64$-inch holes, and secure the keep plate to the door jamb. Close the door and check the surface bolt engagement.

Door Security

The next two styles will restrict the door from opening completely: the security door guard and the door chain. The advantage to these is that the door can be opened slightly to speak to someone on the outside of the door and still have major restriction from the door being opened wide enough for entry. They each have selective pieces that mount to the inside surface of the exterior door, and the mating parts will mount onto the interior door trim.

SECURITY DOOR LOCK INSTALLATION

1 Locate the desired height of the security door guard above the exterior lockset, approximately 60 inches above the floor.

2 Lay out the holes on the jamb/casing face, using the base as a template, drill three 3/32-inch holes, and fasten the three screws supplied.

3 Lay out the holes on the inside surface of the exterior door, drill four 3/32-inch holes, and fasten with the four screws provided.

DOOR CHAIN INSTALLATION

1 Locate the desired height of the door chain above the exterior lockset, approximately 60 inches above the floor.

2 Locate the holes, using the door chain slide plate 1/4-inch back from the door edge on the inside surface of the exterior door, drill four 5/64-inch holes, and attach using the four screws provided.

3 Locate the holes, using the door chain plate, drill two 5/64-inch holes on the door casing, and attach using the two screws provided.

If the exterior door does not have glass to view the outside through, then installing a door viewer is a very good idea. These viewers allow the person on the inside of the door to see who may be at the door and then can decide if they need to open the door or not.

DOOR VIEWER INSTALLATION

1 Locate and drill a 9/16-inch hole through the door at the desired height location, approximately 60 inches above the floor.

2 Disassemble the door viewer and insert the lens part through the hole on the outside surface of the exterior door.

3 Insert the barrel of the door viewer through the hole on the inside surface of the exterior door, and screw both pieces together.

These are relatively easy to install with the use of a drill and the prescribed drill bit. The best height to install these at is approximately 5 feet on center above the inside floor height.

Chapter 6 | Exterior Doors

EXTERIOR DOOR WEATHER STRIPPING

SKILL LEVEL

- Basic

TOOLS REQUIRED

- Hacksaw
- 2-inch putty knife or straight screwdriver
- Hammer
- Door jack to secure the door

MATERIALS REQUIRED

- New door bottom seal or inside-mounted door sweep

Exterior door weather stripping provides protection from the elements and helps maintain the conditioned air inside the home, where it belongs!

One of the most affected areas of the door's weather stripping is the door bottom seal. Many older wooden doors were made with the door bottom seal in the threshold, but this became problematic because people would step on the threshold, causing the rubber seal to become worn, torn, or missing. This would leave a large air gap at the bottom of the door. Doors manufactured today will have the door seal attached to the bottom of the door. Due to the high traffic of people opening and closing the door frequently to enter and exit, the door bottom seal can wear out.

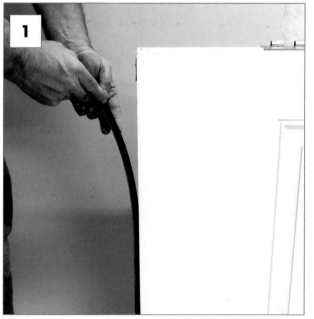

1 Remove the door from the hinges by removing the hinge pins and place the door on the floor on its edge. If a second person is not available, place the door into a door jack to support it. Remove the old door bottom seal by prying at one end and pulling it off.

2 Remove the new door bottom seal from the packaging and make sure that the slotted screw holes are used for attaching the seal to the inside of the door with the packaged screws. When installed correctly, the exterior of the door bottom seal will have the solid flange and drip edge on the exterior of the door.

3 Slide the new door bottom seal over the bottom of the door and mark the seal to the correct length, matching the width of the door.

4 Use a hacksaw to cut the seal to the correct length.

5 Attach the new door bottom seal to the door with the screws included. Be sure to place the screws in the middle of the slot to allow for adjustment when the door is reinstalled in the frame.

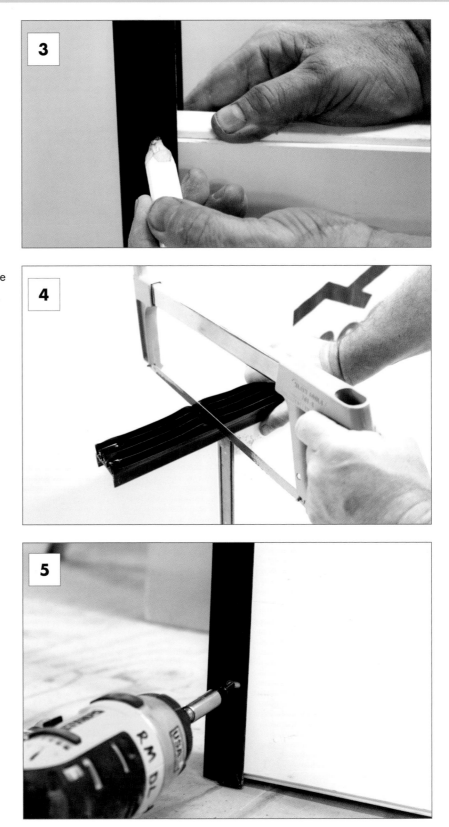

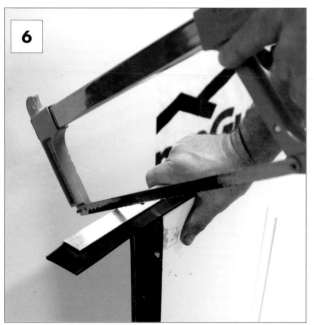

6 If the original door did not include a door bottom seal, but the door seals when closed over a threshold rubber seal, then you can add an aluminum door sweep to the inside of the door at the bottom. Remove the door from the hinges by removing the hinge pins and place the door on the floor on its edge. If a second person is not available, place the door into a door jack for support. Mark the aluminum door sweep to length by holding it against the door bottom edge. Carefully cut to length using a hacksaw.

7 Attach the aluminum door sweep to the bottom inside of the door, using the screws included. Be sure to place the screws in the center of the slots to provide adjustment of the sweep after installing the door.

Exterior door weather stripping also encompasses the use of door seals attached to the wood jamb that create a seal when the door is closed. These door seals include three pieces: two long ones for the vertical sides of the doorjamb, and a shorter one for the horizontal head of the doorjamb. These pieces are held in place by the ribbed design of the compression rubber in the slot of the doorjamb made to secure the weather stripping.

Another area of the exterior door that has a tendency to leak air is the bottom of the door corners where the side jambs meet the door threshold. Self-adhesive vinyl gaskets are made to help seal these areas at each end of the threshold. To attach these self-adhesive gaskets to the bottom of the doorjamb just above the threshold, remove the release paper on the back. Place the gasket on the threshold with the narrow end of the gasket facing the door. This is to allow the gasket to be properly compressed when the door is closed. Note: If the gasket is installed in reverse, the thick end will buckle the gasket when the door is closed. Be sure that the gasket with the thin end facing the door also laps under the vertical rubber compression door seal to provide a "no-gap" installation.

✓ TIP

If the gasket is installed in reverse, the thick end will buckle the gasket when the door is closed. Be sure that the gasket with the thin end facing the door also laps under the vertical rubber compression door seal to provide a "no-gap" installation.

Exterior Door Weather Stripping

ELECTRIC GARAGE DOOR OPENERS

SKILL LEVEL

- Basic

TOOLS REQUIRED

- Stepladder

MATERIALS REQUIRED

- 9-volt battery
- Light bulb(s) (maximum 60 watts)

Electric garage door openers have been in existence for many years. The earlier models consisted of a motor, chain, and track to pull the door up and push it down when the motor was activated by a power button. Today's garage door openers and doors are much improved in design, with quiet operations and mandatory child-safety features.

Battery door for keypad-type garage door opener.

Information regarding current manufacturers and operating and maintenance instructions can be obtained online if a manual for the model being used is not available.

Starting outside, there will be either a key switch or a security push-button numeric keypad. If the outside switch is a key switch, and only one key is available, have copies made of the original key. If the outside switch is a security push-button numeric keypad, it operates with a 9-volt battery. Locate the battery door and remove it to access the 9-volt battery.

The inside switch may be a simple doorbell-style push button or a lockout security-type push button. To deactivate the door from operating, engage the lockout button to "lock," located on the push-button. To reactivate the door, switch the lockout button to "unlock." This feature is another way to ensure that the door cannot be opened while you are away from home for longer periods of time. If the electric door opener style does not have this feature, you can accomplish the same thing by simply unplugging the opener from the electrical receptacle. Remember to plug the opener back in when you return home.

Indoor switch for garage door.

From about the mid-1990s and onward, child-safety electronic sensors have been attached to new electric garage doors. These sensors send an LED beam across the bottom of the door opening between them. When the LED beam is broken by an object or a person and the door is closing, the door will automatically reverse to the opening operation and stop in the fully open position. It will remain fully open until the obstruction is cleared, the beam is sent between the sensors, and the button is pushed to close the door. This is extremely important to remember for two reasons. First, it will keep children from being struck by a closing garage door. Second, anything that falls and blocks the LED beam while you are driving away from your house will leave the door open and your home possibly accessible. I highly recommended that you observe the door in the fully closed position before driving away.

Sensor to prevent damage or injury.

Emergency release.

1 Another feature that every electric garage door opener today has is an emergency release. This release will allow the garage door to operate as a stand-alone door even when the opener is not working properly. To engage the emergency door release in either the up or down position, pull the rope handle toward the opener. This will allow the door hardware attached to the opener track to disengage. The door will then operate as any other door would, able to be opened and closed manually.

2 To connect the door back to the track mechanism, pull the emergency latch rope away from the opener. Slide the door so the attaching hardware will reengage the track hardware and the door will operate with the opener again.

3 On each side of the door should be a deadbolt slide latch, which will need to be engaged in the slots of the vertical door track when the door is operating in the stand-alone mode only. An older door with an opener added to it will probably still have the door latching bars and handle attached. Use these to lock the door securely during stand-alone operation. Every garage door, when closed and attached to the opener, will position the emergency release mechanism vertically just inside the closed door. It is possible to push the top panel in enough to have a thin wire with a loop and pull the emergency release, thereby disengaging the door from the opener.

4 To keep unwanted entrances through the garage door when you leave for extended periods of time, I highly recommended using the manual lock system on the door. Also, disconnecting the plug from the outlet for the opener, so that the opener is not activated with the manual lock system engaged, will prevent damage to the motor. I know this is true from experience. Buying a new control board for the opener because I forgot to disengage the manual locks before operating the opener was expensive!

5 The lights that turn on automatically when the opener is activated can be serviced easily. Locate the push-button tabs on the side or top of the lens to disengage the lens. Remove the lens and place it in a safe location. Replace the bulb(s) with the correct wattage and type of light bulb. Reinstall the lens and check the bulb(s) for correct operation.

6 Most models of electric garage doors include remote opener(s) for use inside the vehicle. These units operate using battery power. Consult the existing unit or manual for the correct battery size and type.

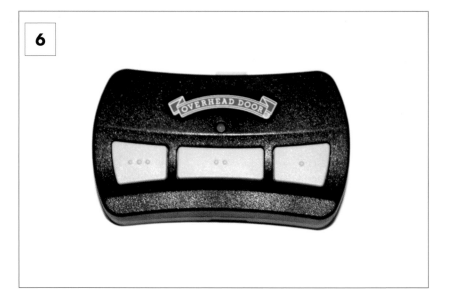

Electric Garage Door Openers

CHAPTER 7
WINDOWS

WINDOW LOCKS

SKILL LEVEL

- Basic

TOOLS REQUIRED

- Slotted or #2 Phillips screwdriver
- Scissors

MATERIALS REQUIRED

- Vinyl self-adhesive seal
- Sash cam lock (if worn)
- Cotton rope for counterweight wood windows

Windows provide the home with daylight, ventilation, and, in some cases, spectacular views of the outside. In the late fall and early spring, southwest-facing windows have the advantage of providing solar heat gain on a sunny day.

To obtain the maximum benefit of windows, homes will seldom have them on the north side. North-facing windows do not get the sun shining through them, only the chilly northern wind blowing against them.

To understand the effects of windows that have performance issues, we need to examine the parts of the window. This will help explain how to improve any deficiencies and make the windows perform better.

The issues we are looking for with an underperforming window are cold air leaks and drafts, condensation buildup on the inside glass surface, and rattling when the wind blows.

The most common type of window installed in a home is the double-hung window. This window provides great ventilation because both the top and bottom sashes are able to open. Most of the time, you will lift the bottom sash to create an air opening; however, having the top sash open is a great advantage for air exchange without the air coming directly into the bottom of the window.

To lock or unlock a double-hung window, locate the sash cam lock(s) at the point where the top and bottom sash meet. These are called the *meeting rails;* narrow double-hung windows will have one sash cam lock, and windows over 30 inches wide will use two sash cam locks. To unlock the sash cam lock, place your fingers on the end of the lock and pull on the handle until the sash cam lock is in the unlocked position. Note: When two sash cam locks are used, they operate parallel to each other.

When the window is unlocked, it can be a challenge to get older windows to open. This is because old wooden top and bottom sashes will swell when they absorb moisture through cracks in the exterior paint. There is no need to worry, though, as there is a tried-and-true method to open them.

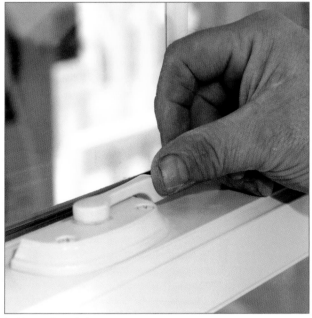

Locking a sash cam lock.

To unstick a bottom sash, place your fist on the top of the bottom sash meeting rail and pound down on the rail. Do this at each end of the meeting rail as well as the center. The pounding produces vibrations that can help shake the bottom sash to release it from the window jamb or any paint that has cured after being painted.

To open the bottom sash after it has been unstuck by your fist, carefully apply steady pressure to the window sash top or bottom rail and lift the window. If the window doesn't move, repeat the process of using your fist on the top rail to unstick the sash. Note: It is possible to separate wooden window sash rails by simply pushing the top meeting rail very hard if the window is stuck.

The top sash can become stuck in the same manner as the bottom sash. To unstick the top sash, open the bottom sash and locate your fist under the bottom meeting rail of the top sash. Pound upward with your fist on the bottom meeting rail at both ends and the middle. After the top sash has been unstuck, use your fingers to grab the top sash and apply steady downward pressure until the top sash pulls down.

After the windows are unstuck and operating fairly freely, check the operation of the sash cam lock. If the lock seems to close extremely easily, it probably needs to be replaced with a new one. The greater the gap at the top and bottom of the window sashes, and the sash cam lock resembles a wedge to take up the gaps and move the top and bottom sashes. Older sash cam locks will not be able to accomplish this because they are worn.

Use the appropriate screwdriver to loosen and remove the sash cam lock screws attaching the sash cam lock to the bottom sash meeting rail, as well as the sash cam lock strike plate on the upper window sash.

Unsticking a bottom sash.

Unsticking a top sash.

Unscrewing sash cam lock from bottom sash.

Unscrewing sash cam lock from top sash.

Chapter 7 | Windows

Window Locks

WINDOW WEATHER STRIPPING

Double-hung windows have three sealing points to stop the air from coming in from the outside. They are located at the top of the upper sash, between the bottom and top meeting rails of the two sashes, and at the bottom of the bottom sash. If these become worn, defective, or missing, you can replace them with a self-adhesive vinyl seal kit.

Lift the bottom sash all the way up and pull the top sash all the way down to expose the seal at the middle meeting rails. If it is worn, missing, or torn, replace it with a self-adhesive vinyl seal. With the top sash still pulled down,

stand on a stepstool or ladder to examine the condition of the top sash seal. If it is worn, missing, or torn, replace it with a self-adhesive vinyl seal. Raise the bottom sash all the way back up to its full open position and kneel down slightly to view the vinyl seal of the bottom sash. If it is worn, missing, or torn, replace it with a self-adhesive seal.

When new vinyl seals are installed at these locations, the sash cam lock should appear to close but will require more finger pressure to fully close. If not, this is an indication the sash cam lock is extremely worn and needs to be replaced.

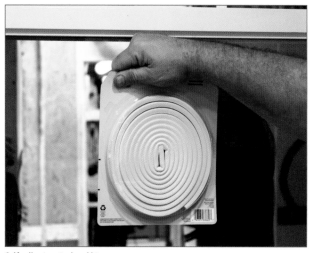

Self-adhesive vinyl seal kit.

Replace worn, missing, or torn seals.

OLDER WINDOW COUNTERWEIGHTS

Windows that were made before World War II utilize a counterweight system attached to a cotton rope. One rope end is installed in a rope groove, with the end of the rope knotted and nailed into a round recess along the side of the top and bottom sashes.

The window frames also have steel pulleys recessed in the top of the window jamb, with two on each side. The pulley closest to the room

Counterweight system for windows made before World War II.

side is for the bottom sash, and the pulley closest to the top window sash is for the top sash.

The other end of the rope is attached to the cast weight that is located inside the window jamb in the weight pocket. There are two cast weights for every sash. This balances the counterweight required to hold the window open. This weight travels downward when the sash is raised and is not designed to bottom out in the weight pocket of the side jamb, so the cotton rope is always under tension.

Because the ropes are under constant tension, the ropes will develop wear spots on them from the pulleys; over extended periods of time, the ropes will break. Generally, only one of the two ropes will break, but that's not a guarantee! If a rope breaks, you will have to locate and remove the window weight-pocket access door on the side of the jamb as well as the window sash stops from the frame on the inside (*never* from the outside). Purchase new cotton rope that matches the existing size that broke. Copy the attachment end of the old rope to the window sash, cut the correct rope length needed, and attach the last end to the hole at the top of the cast weight.

Window frame pulleys.

Remove access door to replace a broken rope.

Attach cast weight to new rope.

Older Window Counterweights

CHAPTER 8

ELECTRIC

ELECTRICAL REPAIRS AND REPLACEMENTS

In this chapter, we will discuss the several types of electrical components and devices that comprise the electrical systems in most homes.

The key to being successful with electrical repairs is to work safely and within the means of your experience. The list of replacement categories in this chapter are meant to be the types of items that we replace or repair regularly in a home. It is *not* intended as a guide for new construction, remodeling, or major repairs.

Electricity in homes is supplied by a transformer on a utility pole or pad-mounted transformer on or near the property. Power from this electric source is carried over service cable wires either overhead or underground to your property.

The power is connected to an electric meter outside to register the number of kilowatts used in a billing cycle. The power is then connected to a main breaker or fuse box inside.

Individual circuits controlled by either a circuit breaker or fuse are run to each room or area of the building to supply current to switches, receptacles, lights, and appliances.

To understand the current available in each property, we must determine the size of the main breaker or fuse.

In much older homes, it is still common to have a main fuse of 60 amps. This type of system is very old and probably has outlived its service life. Caution: Any repairs having this type of service would require the experience of an electrician as these older wires and fuses are extremely easy to overload and may possibly cause fires.

A 100-amp main breaker or fuse is a service that still has some age on its service life but can be reliable and safe if only replacement repairs are made.

The most common service available today is the 200-amp main breaker service. This service has been in existence since the 1970s when the all-electric house was designed and built. This service type has undergone the most extensive code revisions of all three types listed and will be in existence for some time to come.

Breakers versus Fuses

Any electrical system that has fuses as the control element to stop the flow of current to devices and appliances must be worked on with extreme caution when replacing fuses. The most crucial factors are *the correct type and amperage* of fuse(s) being replaced. There is no room for "this will probably work" or "I'll use this one until I get the right one." That is how most electrical fires start in older homes. In addition, most older homes do not have as many individual circuits or outlets per room, so people use extension cords, which can get overloaded, too.

Breakers are devices that will trip when the breaker determines that there is an overload of power flowing from the main panel through the breaker to the circuit. They will also trip when a dead short occurs in the circuit. They offer protection in cases such as a bare ground wire touching a conductor of the power feed line attached to the breaker.

The most important thing to know about a breaker is that you need to reset it until it locks in the on position but *do not hold it in the on position.* Holding it in the on position will not permit the breaker to open in the case of another problem detected in the circuit, which will allow the wires to become overheated and cause a fire.

To understand the wires that comprise an electrical circuit in a home, we must understand the size and type of wires used in the past and today.

Homes built before the 1950s have wires called knob and tube. These wires are individual insulated wires that are installed in the building and use porcelain knobs attached with spikes to the frame as connection points to branch the individual wires to different switches and receptacles. This electrical system is absent of any ground wires, so you must take extreme care when working with it. It is impossible to find the type and style of old switches and receptacles used in these homes, so you must select replacement devices carefully to ensure that the new devices will fit properly in the existing device box. Caution: Turn the power off to remove the electrical device so you can take the device with you to the home-supply center to match the device with the correct replacement.

With the increase in demand of homes being purchased by veterans returning from World War II, every building trade and material type used had to be improved to keep up with the demand. For the electrical industry, the use of sheathed cables was introduced. The same two wire conductors—one black insulated and one white insulated—were placed in a woven sheathed cable jacket so that electricians could install both wires at the same time. These cables also did not include ground wires.

With the improvement of electronics and electrical appliances, it was determined that a grounding system needed to be added to the electrical wiring systems of homes. This was done by adding a bare copper ground wire in the sheathed cable jacket between the one black insulated and one white insulated wire conductors. This allowed all metal electrical boxes and individual switches, receptacles, and appliances to have a dedicated ground wire that would be connected to the ground on which the building sits.

The wire size, or gauge, used for individual circuits in a home has not changed much over the years. What has changed is that the appliances used today are either new in concept and design or are of higher efficiency so as to use significantly less electricity than their previous counterparts.

- **General lighting and light-duty circuits** are 14-gauge with ground wires connecting to 15-ampere breakers.
- **Basement, bathroom, kitchen, garage, and outdoor circuits** are 12-gauge with ground wires connecting to 20-ampere breakers.
- **Kitchen-appliance, refrigerator, dishwasher, garbage-disposal, and microwave circuits** are 12-gauge with ground wires connecting to 20-ampere breakers.

Specialty appliances, such as washing machines and dryers, furnaces, air handlers, water heaters, and outdoor condensing units, require the experience of qualified service technicians, but we will cover preventative maintenance of these items.

ELECTRICAL TOOLS

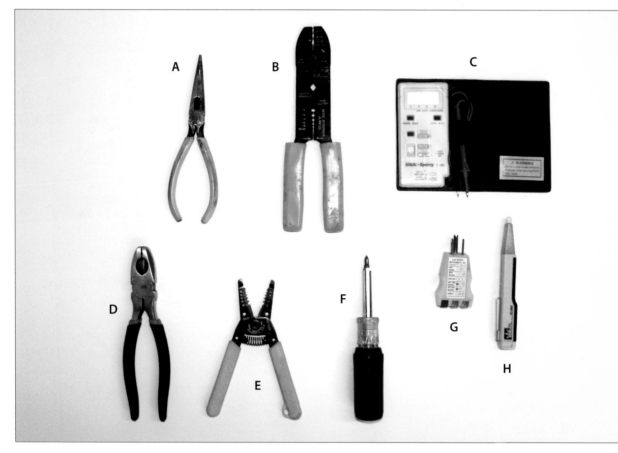

Tools of the electrical trade are unique for each application, and the most common types are shown above. It is so tempting to use your grandfather's older-style tools. I guarantee you that they are in impeccable shape. However, they probably lack the handle insulation required today to protect the user *if, by accident,* the tool comes in contact with a live wire or conductor and a ground.

You must use extreme caution when working with metal tool ends around electricity. You do not want to experience the scare of what resembles welding sparks when any metal tool end comes in contact with a live wire and a ground connection. I have a few tools in my box that have those scars of mistakes on them!

Most electrical replacements and repairs that you do will involve these tools. Understanding the function of each tool will provide you with the easiest method and best results for the task at hand.

(top, left to right)

A - insulated needle-nose pliers
B - insulated terminal crimp
C - digital electrical meter

(bottom, left to right)

D - insulated lineman's pliers
E - insulated wire stripper
F - insulated four-way screwdriver
G - polarity plug tester
H - noncontact electrical tester

Chapter 8 | Electric

A digital electric meter.

Insulated wire strippers.

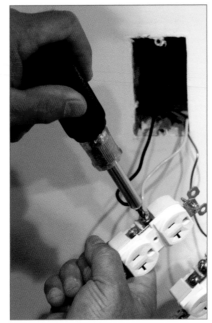

An insulated four-way screwdriver.

A polarity plug tester indicating a correct wiring sequence.

Insulated needle-nose pliers are designed to cut individual wires, attaching to parts in tight spaces and looping wire ends if a wire stripper is not available.

An **insulated terminal crimp** is designed to cut individual wires, strip insulation from individual wires, and crimp wire terminals onto the wire ends.

A **digital electric meter** is designed to measure AC and DC current, resistance of wires (ohms), and circuit continuity. These meters operate on a watch battery and must be manually turned on and off.

Insulated lineman pliers are designed to cut wires, straighten bent wire ends, and twist stripped wire ends for wire nut caps and bare copper ground wires before crimping with a copper sleeve.

Insulated wire strippers are designed to cut wires, stripping insulation from designated wire gauge sizes. They can also be used to bend loops at the stripped ends of wire for attaching to the device screw terminals.

An **insulated four-way screwdriver** is designed to tighten and loosen #1 and #2 Phillips-head and slotted-head screws.

CAUTION

Any LED light sequence other than **correct** needs to be addressed immediately.

A **polarity plug tester** is designed to monitor the correct wiring sequence of 120-volt duplex receptacles. LED lights will turn on when power is present at the receptacle and the tester is plugged in. The tester legend label indicates the following conditions:

- Open ground
- Open neutral
- Open hot
- Hot/ground reverse
- Hot/neutral reverse
- Correct

A **noncontact electrical tester** is designed to detect electrical current flowing at or near an electrical switch, receptacle, junction box, or exposed cable. These testers are preferred for safety and ease of detecting whether current is present or has been interrupted by removing the fuse or turning off the breaker at the power source.

A great way to purchase proper electrical hand tools in good used condition is to visit your local flea market or search online at the many sites used to sell personal items. Before you purchase, make sure that any used tool is in good, safe operating condition. Too many injuries and accidents occur because people used tools that should have been discarded. You can also damage your project if a tool slips because it has outlived its useful life.

ELECTRICAL CONNECTIONS

Using the correct electrical-connection component is crucial for the function and safety of the circuit. Everyone knows that a 1-inch round peg won't fit into a 1-inch square hole, and the same principles apply to electrical-connection components. Can I use a wire nut cap designed for larger wire capacities for a much smaller wire capacity? Maybe? Should I? *Absolutely not!* If you use parts for purposes other than what they were designed for, the integrity and/or safety of the circuit will be jeopardized.

MULTIPLE SWITCHES/RECEPTACLES

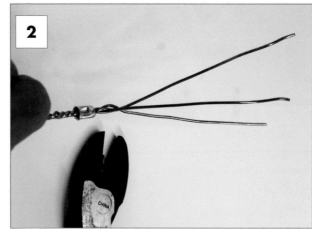

1 Use bare ground crimps when a device box has multiple cables with multiple switches and/or receptacles. The circuit requires all grounds to be twisted together in a clockwise direction. Use lineman's pliers to accomplish this.

2 Each device requires a bare ground wire attached to each device's green ground terminal screw. Accomplish this by leaving individual bare copper conductors past the uninsulated ground crimp.

SINGLE SWITCH/RECEPTACLE

1 The use of an insulated green ground wire nut cap is used when a device box has multiple cables with only one switch or receptacle. The circuit requires all grounds to be twisted together in a clockwise direction. Use lineman's pliers to accomplish this. Only one ground wire is attached to the green ground screw terminal of the device. This is accomplished by leaving only one bare copper conductor to pass through the hole in the top of the cap. The wire nut cap is tightened by hand in a clockwise direction.

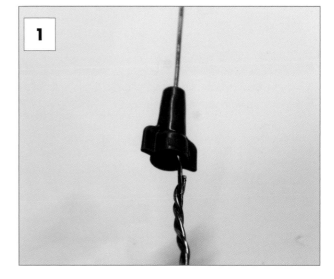

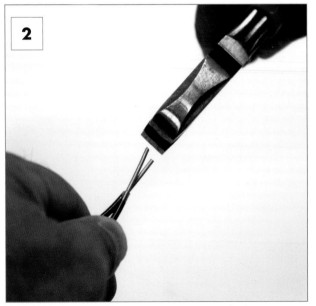

2 When using a wire nut cap to connect multiple wires together, be very careful with the insulation strip length of each wire. To provide the proper number of twists using lineman's pliers, I recommend a 1-inch strip length.

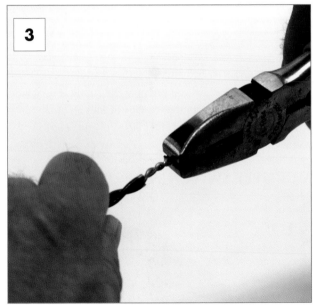

3 Complete a minimum of three twists in a clockwise direction to join the bare conductors of insulated wires.

4 Trim the twisted bare wire connection to a minimum of ½-inch long with the lineman's pliers.

5 Place the open end of the insulated wire nut cap over the cut end of the joined wires. Tighten the wire nut cap by hand-twisting in a clockwise direction. The wire nut caps have a spring inside to act as a threaded tapered nut and grab the twisted wires.

CAUTION

Never rely only on the wire nut twisting action to create a tight, safe connection. It can become a loose connection over time as the wire nut cap unwinds itself.

Chapter 8 | Electric

Electrical Connections

REMOVING CONDUCTOR INSULATION WITH WIRE STRIPPERS

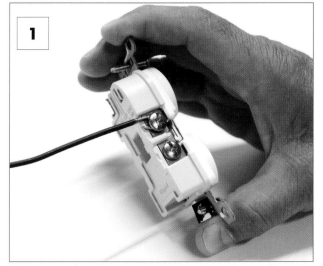

1 Using insulated wire strippers to remove the conductor insulation from a black, white, or red wire to attach to a screw terminal of a switch or receptacle can be tricky. Strip ¾ inch of insulation from the end of the wire. Check this using the bare wire gauge on the back of the device.

Cap Colors

Each color wire nut cap has a specific wire size as well as a specific number of wires with which it can be joined for a safe and reliable wire connection. A chart for each color is printed on the packaging.

- **Yellow** can be used for 14-2 and 14-3 AWG conductors.

- **Red** can be used for 12-2 and 12-3 AWG conductors.

- **Orange** can be used for 16-2 and 18-2 AWG conductors.

2 Place the stripped wire end into the hole in the jaw of the wire strippers with approximately ⅛ to ³⁄₁₆ inch sticking out of the back of the jaw.

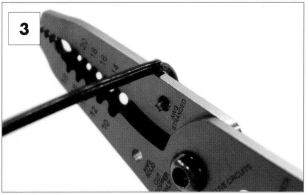

3 Rotate the strippers to create a 180-degree open loop.

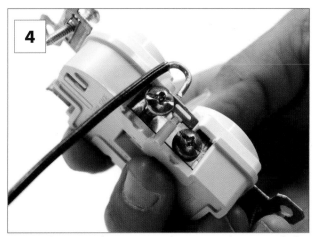

4 Attach wire to the corresponding terminal screw with the loop in a clockwise direction and tighten by hand with a screwdriver.

CHAPTER 9

ELECTRICAL DEVICE REPAIRS

(left to right) front images of GFCI 15 amp; duplex 15 amp.

Electric receptacles are divided into several categories according to their end use and wire-gauge connections. It is always tempting, when rushed or confused, to mix receptacle types.

Older receptacles from the 1950s and 1960s do not have the capability of a dedicated ground connection, nor can they have polarized plugs inserted into them. With the sophisticated high-power electronics of today's era, both of these improved aspects of the receptacles are required for personal safety and equipment protection.

The original ground fault receptacles were labeled ground fault interruptor (GFI). These receptacles were designed to protect the user against electrical hazards where water was present, such as at sinks and outdoor locations.

As improvements were made to the devices, their label was changed to ground fault circuit interruptor (GFCI). They became required in/near garages, electric panels, basements, and pools, in addition to sinks and outdoor locations, giving residents the best possible shock-hazard protection.

We do not use GFCI devices at garbage disposals, refrigerator/freezers, washing machines, or sump pump locations because if they are tripped, the appliances to which they are connected will no longer have power to operate. Imagine coming home after a long weekend to find a refrigerator or freezer full of warm food or a basement filled with water because the sump pump didn't automatically turn on during the heavy downpour.

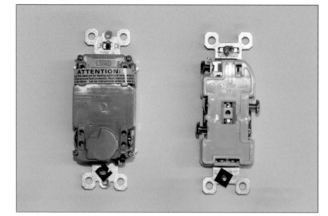

(left to right) rear images of GFCI 15 amp; duplex 15 amp.

The various types of duplex receptacles are shown in the photos above. When purchasing receptacle replacements, remember to match the color, voltage, and amperage that is currently being used.

Chapter 9 | Electrical Device Repairs

DUPLEX RECEPTACLES

SKILL LEVEL

- Skilled

TOOLS REQUIRED

- Noncontact electrical tester
- Polarity plug tester
- Four-way screwdriver
- Lineman's pliers
- Wire strippers
- Torpedo level

MATERIALS REQUIRED

- New receptacle that matches the existing one

Receptacles can go bad due to the way they were originally installed, the wear and tear on the plug contacts that allow plugs to loosen, or a broken face at the ground lug. A receptacle that was originally wired through the back connection holes instead of having the wires looped around the side terminal screws will lose electrical connections over an extended period of time. This can be hazardous because arching can occur behind the receptacle.

Each electrical receptacle being replaced must match the style, color, voltage, and amperage capacity. This information will be listed on the shelf tag at the home-supply center or on the box label.

For **general-duty** receptacles, we will use 125 volts/15 amps attached to 14-gauge wires connected to 15-ampere breakers or fuses. These receptacles are generally found in hallways, living rooms, bedrooms, and family rooms.

For **special-duty** receptacles, we will use 125 volts/20 amps attached to 12-gauge wires connected to 20-ampere breakers or fuses. These receptacles are found in kitchens, bathrooms, dining rooms, garages, basements, and outdoors.

Both types of receptacles have two side-mounted brass terminal screws on one side and two silver terminal screws on the opposite side. One green terminal ground screw is located on the silver screw terminal end.

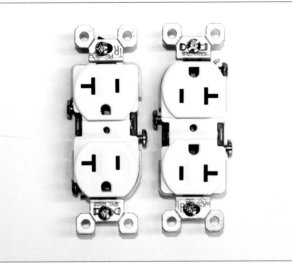

20 amp duplex receptacles.

Duplex receptacle installations for decades have been done with the ground lug facing down for residential homes and the ground lug facing up for commercial installations.

Why the difference? Besides being the accepted practice in each application, the plugs found on heavier-duty equipment and medical devices have a three-prong plug. The ground lug of the three-prong is the longest prong and, therefore, when a plug is loose or beginning to come out of the receptacle, the ground is the last connection lost. Therefore, the equipment is grounded almost until the plug completely falls out.

Now, you are probably wondering why, on newer residential receptacles, the ground lug is facing up. Did a commercial electrician install one that way out of habit? The answer is most likely not. When a three-prong plug is inserted into a receptacle and becomes loose with the ground lug facing down, it creates a shock hazard for anyone, especially small children. The hot and neutral plug prongs are exposed and therefore anything conductive that comes in contact with them simultaneously creates a shock hazard and/or electrical short.

Placing the ground lug upward, the same way as commercial receptacles, provides for the ground connection to be the last lost connection when a plug is pulled out, and the ground prong acts as a pivot point for any object that falls onto the partially-pulled-out plug. The object will most likely fall on the floor instead of creating an electrical hazard or short.

1 First, turn off the power that is being supplied to the receptacle circuit you are replacing. Use a noncontact tester to make sure that the power is off. Next, remove the cover plate. Place the cover plate screw back into the threaded hole of the original receptacle so it doesn't become lost.

2 Unscrew the two device screws that secure the receptacle to the device box. Pull the receptacle out from the face of the wall. There should be a minimum of 6 inches of wires folded behind the receptacle to allow this. The existing wires will help support the receptacle in the air, and the new receptacle can be held beside the existing one.

CAUTION

To be sure that you correctly identified the breaker or fuse at the power source location, insert a plug of an electrical device, such as a portable radio or light. The device should not operate if the correct circuit was turned off.

Chapter 9 | Electrical Device Repairs

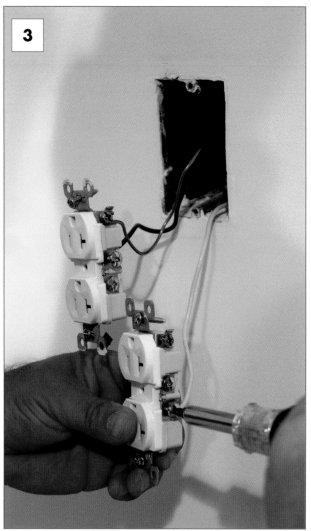

4 Caution: In the event that the wires are inserted into the back of the existing device, cut them flush with the back of the existing receptacle. An alternative is to use a piece of wire, which can be inserted into the hole next to the wire, and then release the wire from the spring connection inside the receptacle. This type of wire connection is *not preferred* for safe and long-lasting wire connections for the receptacle. The cut wires will require the proper strip length of insulation matched with the strip gauge on the back of the receptacle.

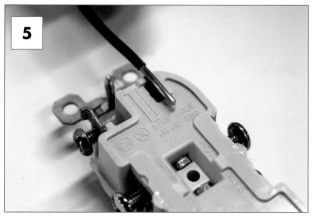

3 With the ground lugs of the receptacles and the green ground screws facing the same direction, remove one wire at a time from the existing receptacle and attach each wire to the corresponding terminal screw of the new receptacle. The **black** wires must be connected to the **brass** screws. The **white** wires must be connected to the **silver** screws. The **bare** ground wire must be connected to the green ground screw. Be sure that the wire loops are in a clockwise direction; this is required when the terminal screws are tightened for the best electrical connections. Note: All duplex receptacles have the side terminal screws turned out fully. Tighten all four screws even if only two have wires connected to them.

5 Then, bend a loop in the bare wire to attach it to the corresponding terminal screws. *Only tighten terminal screws by hand to ensure proper tightening of each.* Carefully fold the excess wire back into the device box and secure the new receptacle with the attached device screws to the device box.

6 Make sure the receptacle is vertical by using a torpedo level. Place the existing cover plate over the new receptacle. Remove the cover plate screw from the original removed receptacle and secure the cover plate with the screw. For a professionally installed appearance, the slots of the screws should be horizontal. Restore power to the receptacle circuit at the breaker or fuse location. Use a polarity tester to be sure that all of the wires are correctly connected to allow for polarity plugs that are used to supply current to sophisticated electronics. The polarity plug tester has a legend label to correspond to the three LED lights that indicate the condition of the receptacle wiring. Two yellow lights on in a row indicate that the wires are correct.

GFCI RECEPTACLES

The original ground fault receptacles were labeled as GFI. These receptacles were designed to protect the user against electrical hazards where water is present at sinks and outdoor locations. These original devices connected the wires using terminal screws like the duplex receptacles.

As improvements were made to the devices, the label was changed to GFCI. The new devices now connect the wires using proper insulation strip length and are installed through the back of the device.

The location requirements in garages and basements or at electric panels, whirlpool tubs, and pools were added to the original sink and outdoor locations, giving the resident the best possible shock hazard protection.

GFCI receptacles generally do not need to be replaced. However, when the internal circuit that detects faults no longer functions, it is time to replace the device. Imagine coming home after a long weekend to find a refrigerator or freezer full of warm food or a basement filled with water because the sump pump didn't automatically turn on during the heavy down-pouring rain.

SKILL LEVEL

- **Skilled**

TOOLS REQUIRED

- **Noncontact electrical tester**
- **Polarity plug tester**
- **Four-way screwdriver**
- **Lineman's pliers**
- **Wire stripper**
- **Torpedo level**

MATERIALS REQUIRED

- **New GFCI receptacle to match the existing one**

CAUTION

We DO NOT use these at garbage disposals, refrigerators, freezers, washing machines, or sump pump locations because, if they are tripped, the appliance they are connected to will no longer have power to it.

GFCI receptacle wire connections are critical for the device to perform correctly. There are one or two sets of wire cables in the device box when the existing receptacle is removed. Many times, the electrician places tags on or otherwise marks the wires as "LINE" and "LOAD," or "FEED-IN" and "FEED-OUT," or "IN" and "OUT." These labels differentiate which wire is coming from the power source and which wire may be continuing on to the next receptacle.

For device boxes with only one cable, the connection to the new device is simple. The connections will be made using the "LINE" half of the receptacle only.

For device boxes with two cables, one cable will be matched and attached to the "LINE" half of the receptacle, while the second cable will be matched and attached to the "LOAD" half of the receptacle.

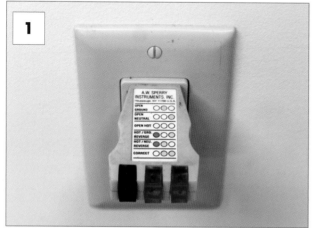

1 First turn off the power that is being supplied to the receptacle circuit you are replacing. The use of a polarity plug tester can be used to assure the power is off. Next, remove the cover plate. Place the cover plate screws back into the threaded holes of the original receptacle so they don't become lost.

CAUTION

To be sure the breaker or fuse was correctly identified at the power source location, insert a plug of an electrical device, such as a portable radio or light. The device should **NOT** operate if the correct circuit was turned off.

2 Unscrew the two device screws that secure the receptacle to the device box.

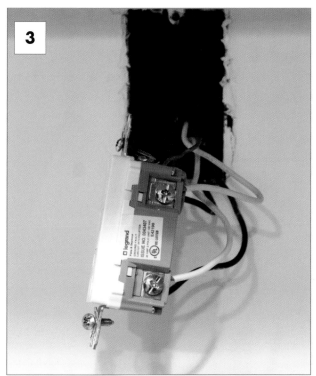

3 Pull the receptacle out from the face of the wall. There should be a minimum of 6 inches of wires folded behind the receptacle to allow this.

4 The existing wires will help support the receptacle in the air and the new receptacle can be held beside the existing one. Match the wording of "LINE" and "LOAD" between the two devices on the back side.

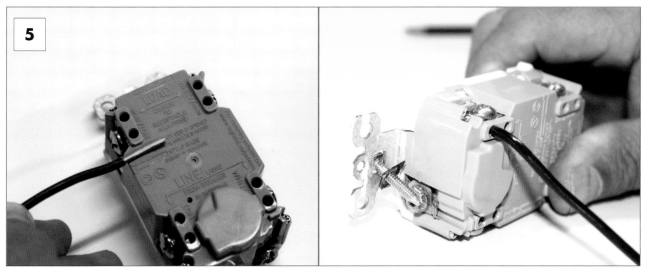

5 Loosen the black wire of the "LINE" half of the existing receptacle. If the old style used the side screw terminal to attach the wire, carefully straighten the wire end with lineman's pliers. Be sure that the wire strip length matches the back strip gage length on the back of the new device and that the loose brass color screw terminal of the new device is facing upward when inserting the black wire into the back "LINE" hole.

Chapter 9 | Electrical Device Repairs

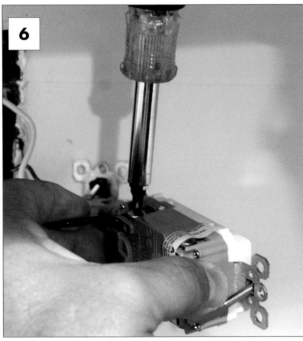

6 When tightening the screw, the wire will be properly connected inside the device. Pull on the wire from the back to be sure the connection is tight and the wire does not pull out.

7 Next, remove the yellow sticker covering the "LOAD" connection terminals.

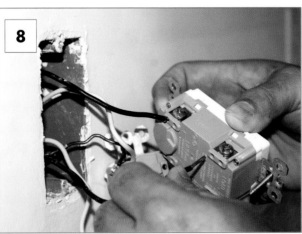

8 Loosen the black wire from the "LOAD" half of the existing receptacle. Follow the same instructions for the correct strip length for the black "LINE" wire. With the receptacle having the loose brass color screw terminal facing on the new device, insert the wire into the back "LOAD" hole. Tighten the terminal screw to secure the wire connection is made.

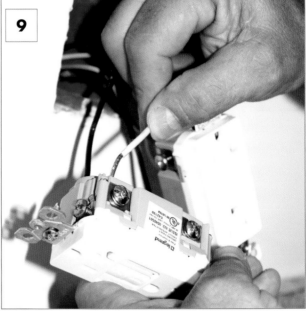

9 Repeat the same process for the white "LINE" and "LOAD" wires, making sure all four wire connections are secure and the wires **DO NOT** pull out from the back of the new device.

Chapter 9 | Electrical Device Repairs

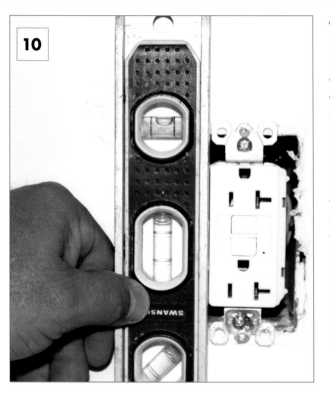

10 Last, remove the bare ground wire from the existing device and attach to the green screw terminal of the new device. Be sure the wire loop, if used, is in the clockwise direction for proper connection. Carefully fold the excess wire back into the device box and secure the new receptacle with the attached device screws to the device box. Make sure the receptacle body is vertical by using a torpedo level. Place the new cover plate, if provided, over the new receptacle. If not, remove the cover plate screws from the original removed receptacle and secure the original cover plate with the two screws. The slots of the screws should be horizontal for that professionally installed appearance. Restore power to the receptacle circuit at the breaker or fuse location. The use of a polarity tester can be used to be sure all of the wires are correctly connected. The polarity plug tester has a legend label to correspond to the three LED lights that indicate the condition of the receptacle wiring. Two yellow lights on in a row (as seen on page 78) indicates the wires are correct.

GFCI receptacles can control up to two additional duplex receptacles in front of them in the circuit. When the GFCI detects an electrical hazard, it will trip immediately. This disrupts current to the other receptacles it is attached to. Knowing which GFCI receptacles control which duplex receptacle in any given circuit can eliminate wasted time in restoring power to the circuit by pushing the RESET button back in.

Caution: If the GFCI receptacle continues to trip, the cause of the electrical fault has to be determined and eliminated. Other than simple normal issues, a qualified electrician will be needed to solve the mystery.

Chapter 9 | Electrical Device Repairs

SINGLE-POLE SWITCHES

SKILL LEVEL

- Skilled

TOOLS REQUIRED

- Noncontact electrical tester
- Four-way screwdriver
- Lineman's pliers
- Wire stripper
- Torpedo level

MATERIALS REQUIRED

- New switch that matches the existing one

Switches rarely will go bad, but occasionally they do. Older switches may have been wired through the back connection holes instead of having the wires looped around the side terminal screws. This can cause a loose electrical connection, which can create arcing of the wires behind the switch.

Each electrical switch being replaced must match the style, color, voltage, and amperage capacity. This information will be listed on the shelf tag at the home-supply center or on the box label.

For general-duty light switches, we will use 125 volts/15 amps attached to 14-gauge wires connected to 15-ampere breakers or fuses.

For special-duty appliance switches, we will use 125 volts/20 amps attached to 12-gauge wires connected to 20-ampere breakers or fuses.

Both types of receptacles have two side-mounted brass terminal screws and one green terminal ground screw.

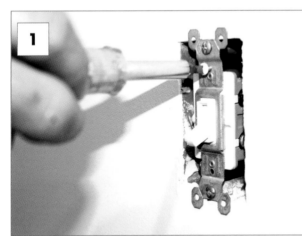

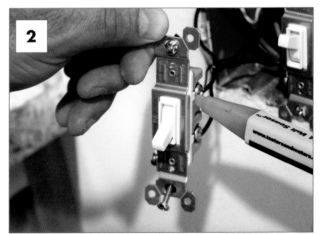

1 First, turn off the power that is being supplied to the switch circuit you are replacing. Use a noncontact tester to ensure that the power is off. Caution: To be sure that you correctly identified the breaker or fuse at the power source location, turn the switch on that normally operated the device. The device should not operate if you turned off the correct circuit. Next, remove the cover plate. Place the cover plate screws back into the threaded holes of the original switch so they don't get lost.

2 Another test method is to touch the noncontact tester near both of the brass terminal screws while flipping the toggle on and off to be sure that current is not flowing to the switch being replaced. Unscrew the two device screws that secure the switch to the device box. Pull the switch out from the face of the wall. There should be a minimum of 6 inches of wires folded behind the switch to allow this. The existing wires will help support the switch in the air, and you can hold the new switch beside the existing one.

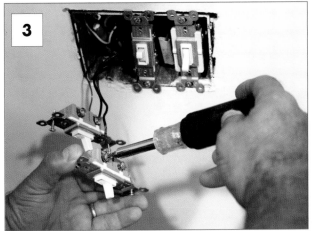

3 With the on/off labeling on the toggles and the green ground screws facing the same direction, remove one wire at a time from the existing switch and attach the wires to the corresponding terminal screws of the new switch. Attach the bare ground wire to the green ground terminal screw. Be sure that the wire loops are in a clockwise direction; this is required when the terminal screws are tightened for the best electrical connections.

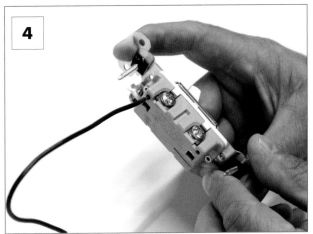

4 Caution: In the event that the wires are inserted into the back of the existing device, cut them flush with the back of the existing switch. An alternative is to use a piece of wire, which can be inserted into the hole next to the wire, and then release the wire from the spring connection inside the switch. This type of wire connection is not preferred for safe and long-lasting wire connections for the switch. The cut wires will require the proper strip length of insulation, using the strip gauge on the back of the device. Then, bend a loop in the bare wire to attach it to the corresponding terminal screw (see page 81).

✓ TIP

Only tighten terminal screws by hand to ensure proper tightening of each.

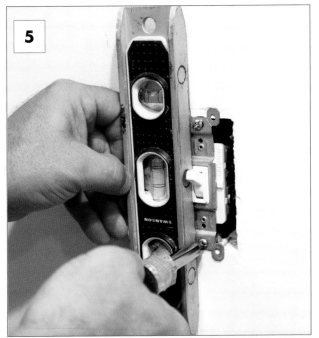

5 Carefully fold the excess wire back into the device box and secure the new switch with the attached device screws to the device box. Make sure that the switch body is vertical by using a torpedo level.

6 Place the existing cover plate over the new switch. Remove the cover plate screws from the original removed switch and secure the cover plate with the two screws. For a professionally installed appearance, the slots of the screws should be vertical.

Chapter 9 | Electrical Device Repairs

THREE-WAY SWITCHES

SKILL LEVEL

- Skilled

TOOLS REQUIRED

- **Noncontact electrical tester**
- **Four-way screwdriver**
- **Lineman's pliers**
- **Wire strippers**

MATERIALS REQUIRED

- **New three-way switch that matches the existing one**

Three-way switches can wear out over time because they are used every time we enter or leave a room that adjoins another room. Each electrical three-way switch being replaced must match the style, color, voltage, and amperage capacity.

General duty three-way light switches require 125 volts/15 amps with two side-mounted terminal screws on one side. One screw is brass and the other screw is black. On the opposite side is one brass screw and one green terminal ground screw.

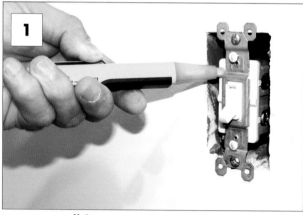

1 First, turn off the power to the three-way switch circuit you are replacing. Use a noncontact tester to make sure that the power is off.

CAUTION

To be sure that you correctly identified the breaker or fuse at the power source location, turn the three-way light switch on at both locations that normally control the light. The light should not operate if the correct circuit was turned off.

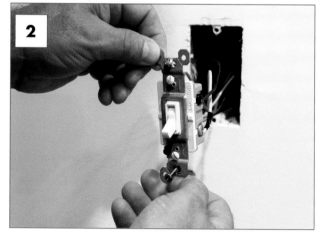

2 Next, remove the cover plate screws and install them in the original switch so they don't get lost later. Unscrew the two device-mounting screws that attach the switch to the device box. Pull the switch out from the face of the wall. There should be a minimum of 6 inches of wires folded behind the switch to allow this.

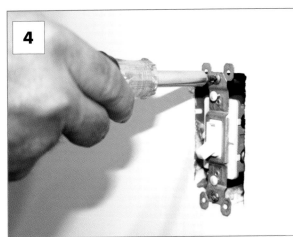

4 The cut wires will require the proper strip length of insulation, using the strip length gauge on the back of the new device. Then, bend a loop in the bare wire to attach it to the corresponding terminal screw. Carefully fold the excess wire back into the device box and attach the screws of the replaced three-way switch in the device box. Check with a torpedo level to be sure that the three-way switch is vertical. Place the existing cover plate over the replaced switch, remove the cover plate screws from the original removed switch, and secure the cover plate with the two screws. For a professionally installed appearance, the slots of the screws should be vertical.

✓ **TIP**

Three-way switches vary from single-pole switches because they use three conductors plus the bare ground wire.

3 The existing wires will help support the switch in the air, and you can hold the new switch beside the existing one. With the dark terminal screws in the same directions, remove one wire at a time from the existing switch and attach each wire to the corresponding terminal screw of the new switch. Attach the bare ground wire to the green ground terminal screw. Be sure that the wire loops are in the clockwise direction; this is required when the terminal screws are tightened for the best connections.

✓ **TIP**

Only tighten terminal screws by hand to ensure proper tightening of each.

CAUTION

In the event that the wires are inserted into the back of the existing device, cut them flush with the back of the existing switch. An alternative is to use a piece of wire, which can be inserted into the hole next to the wire, and then release the wire from the spring connection inside the switch. This type of wire connection is not preferred for safe and long-lasting wire connections for the switch.

Chapter 9 | Electrical Device Repairs

OVER/UNDER SWITCH REPLACEMENTS

SKILL LEVEL

- Skilled

TOOLS REQUIRED

- **Noncontact electrical tester**
- **Four-way screwdriver**
- **Lineman's pliers**
- **Wire stripper**
- **Torpedo level**

MATERIALS REQUIRED

- **New over/under switch to match existing one or circuit requirements for new switch**

The over/under switch has a unique application that allows it to take the place of two independent switches mounted in one device box. The cover plate style for this switch is the same as that for a duplex receptacle.

The internal wiring design allows for one line (power) attached to the switch to control two separate loads (light and fan) independently while saving space in a device box. This is done by the use of a brass bridge between the two line (power) screws. If two separate line wires (power) from two different circuits are in the box, they can be attached to the line (power) screw terminals of the switch also.

The use of a brass bridge attached between the two power screws must be broken to allow for separately controlled circuits.

The switch will have two separately spaced brass terminal screws on one side. These screw terminals are for each of the load (light and fan) to be connected to. There is also one green ground terminal screw.

Over/under switches do not often need to be replaced. What does happen occasionally is that a device, such as a fan/light combination in the bathroom ceiling, is wired to operate both functions with just one switch.

If there is a window in the bathroom, and the natural daylight provides enough light during the day, then every time the fan is turned on, the light is wasting electricity. The same is true at night when you need to use only the light—for example, when washing your hands. At these times, the fan is wasting electricity every time the light is turned on.

1 First, turn off the power to the switch circuit that you are replacing. Use a noncontact tester to ensure that the power is off. *In addition, the switches should not function without power.* Using a flat-head screwdriver, loosen and remove the cover plate screws from the devices. Place the cover plate screws back into the threaded holes of the original devices so they don't get lost. Unscrew the two device-mounting screws that attach the switch to the device box. Pull the switch out from the face of the wall. There should be a minimum of 6 inches of wires folded behind the switch to allow this. The existing wires will help support the switch in the air, and you can hold the new switch beside the existing one.

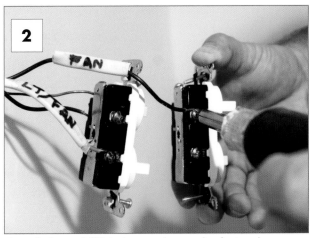

2 With the on/off labeling on the toggles facing the same direction, remove one wire at a time from the existing switch and attach them to the corresponding terminal screws of the new switch.

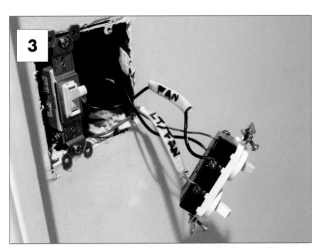

3 Be sure that the wire loops are in the clockwise direction; this is required when the terminal screws are tightened for the best connections. The existing wires may also be labeled to ensure that they are reconnected correctly.

CAUTION

In the event that the wires are inserted into the back of the existing device, cut them flush with the back of the existing switch. An alternative is to use a piece of wire, which can be inserted into the hole next to the wire, and then release the wire from the spring connection inside the switch. This type of wire connection is *not preferred* for safe and long-lasting wire connections for the switch.

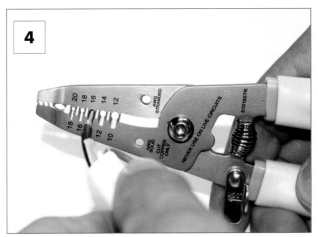

4 The cut wires will require the proper strip length of insulation according to the strip gauge on the back of the device. Then, bend a loop in the bare wire to attach it to the corresponding terminal screw.

✓ TIP

Only tighten terminal screws by hand to ensure proper tightening of each.

Over/Under Switch Replacements

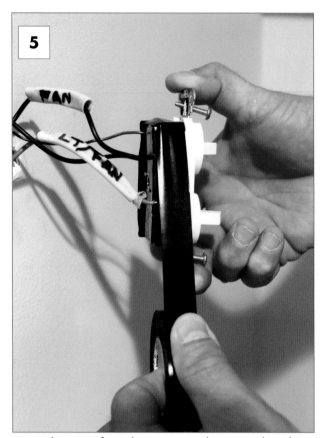

5 On this type of switch, I recommend covering the side screw terminals with electrical tape. Reinstall the new switch and carefully fold the wires back into the device box.

6 Reinstall the cover plate and screws with a flat-head screwdriver; do not overtighten the cover plate screws. The cover plate's screw slots should be vertical, and the over/under switch's screw slots should be horizontal for that professionally installed appearance. After you've completed the replacement, restore power to the circuit and test the function of the switches. If you need to make any corrections, turn off the power to the circuit again before you begin.

Chapter 9 | Electrical Device Repairs

Over/Under Switch Replacements

CHAPTER 10

WATER SERVICE

MUNICIPAL WATER LINE

House water lines can use a variety of sizes and materials to make water connections. Homes built prior to the 1940s may have galvanized water lines, and some can contain lead.

These water lines relied on threaded pipe connections to join pipes and connect fittings. The threads were cut onto the round pipes by the plumbers in the field, which degraded the galvanized plating of the pipes. Hard water from public and private well-water systems would corrode these pipes over their service lifetimes.

After the 1940s, copper became the water line material of choice. The first copper lines installed in many older homes were ⅜ inch in diameter. The ½-inch and ¾-inch copper lines were installed beginning in the late 1950s.

Copper water lines rely on soldered connections to join pipes and connect fittings. The early pipes were soldered using a flux that contained smaller amounts of lead. Today, all solder flux and paste products are lead free.

When attempting to match any water connection to copper, measure the inside pipe diameter to determine whether it is ⅜-, ½- or ¾-inch in size.

In the 1980s, plastic pipe known as CPVC was introduced into market. It has the same connections and pipe sizes as the ½- and ¾-inch copper pipes.

CPVC water lines rely on a primer-cleaner and solvent-based glue to join the pipes as well as connect fittings. The early pipes were glued with a clear solvent-based glue specifically for CPVC products. Today, the solvent adhesive is orange and called "CPVC cement."

In the 1990s, plastic pipe known as PEX was introduced into the market. It has the same connections and pipe sizes as the ½- and ¾-inch copper pipes. In addition, it has many specialty fittings and adapters that are needed to make this system leakproof and efficient.

PEX pipes rely on a manifold system to run continuous individual hot and cold water lines to every faucet and fixture. In this individually run system, the use of Ts and elbows is eliminated, which, in turn, eliminates the chance of leaks behind a wall or above a ceiling. Leaks can, however, still occur if screws and nails installed by others after the lines are run penetrate the continuous water lines.

At both ends of the continuous PEX water lines are connection fittings secured to the pipe with compression rings. These rings are compressed with a specific tool to create the correct crimp size and pressure.

Understanding which piping system or combined systems are in use in the building can go a long way toward diagnosing a problem. If a simple solution is possible, and the parts are available, then you have peace of mind in knowing that water won't be dripping where it shouldn't be.

Water main valve.

Second valve connection.

Water Main Service

Water comes into the property from a public water service that is usually under the street. The water main is connected to a valve in the right of way of the property, usually at the sidewalk or just behind the curb. At this location, you will find a small cast-iron cap with WATER stamped on it. This is where the municipal water technician or a licensed plumber can stop the flow of water between the main service line and the house.

The 1-inch main water line runs from the curbside stop valve into the building to another valve—either a gate valve or ball valve—and then continues to the municipal water meter. A ¾-inch line is connected to the opposite side of the meter, where a second valve connection is made. These two valves are important because the water department can easily replace the meter between these valves if needed.

The ¾-inch line continues to a Tee just above the cold-water connection to the hot-water heater. The bottom of the Tee is connected to the water heater, and the top of the Tee connects to the first faucet in the line of cold-water connections. The hot-water side of the water heater is connected using a ¾-inch line that goes to the first faucet in the line of hot-water connections.

On a public water system, the pressure is normally around 60 psi. This is well below the burst test pressure of water lines, fittings, and valves. Also, the pressure-relief valve for water heaters is factory-set at 75 psi.

WELL SYSTEM

Water comes into the property from a well that is located on the property. The well will have either a submersible pump connected to a 1-inch line near the bottom of the well casing or a jet pump mounted inside the house, usually near the pressure tank. This tank applies the correct amount of pressure to the well water in the system.

A submersible pump located near the bottom of the well casing has a check valve that closes when the pump stops running, so the 1-inch line remains primed and will not interrupt the constant flow of water when the pump turns back on. A jet pump has the same check valve at the bottom of the 1-inch line that is located near the bottom of the well casing and will not interrupt the flow of water when the pump turns back on.

A steel pressure tank located in the house contains a rubber bladder. The bladder is filled with air to a factory setting; the water from the pump enters the pressure tank at the bottom connection, and the rubber bladder is used to apply pressure against the water.

The bladder pressure should be 2 pounds less than the cut-on pressure limit of the pressure switch. With the pressure switch in the "on" position, turn off the breaker to the pressure switch. Drain water from a faucet nearby until you hear the contacts close on the pressure switch. Stop the flow of water from the faucet. Remove the valve stem cap and check the bladder pressure with a tire gauge. The gauge should read 2 pounds lower than the cut-on setting of the pressure switch. If the reading is lower than 2 pounds, add enough air to achieve the 2-pound difference.

Indoor pressure tank.

Checking bladder pressure.

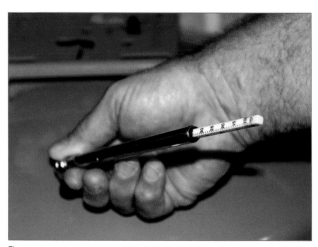

Tire pressure gauge.

A second check valve is installed in the house to the 1-inch Tee of the pressure tank on the pump side of the Tee. This prevents backflow or siphoning of the pressure tank and well line in the event that the check valve near the bottom of the well casing fails. The arrow casts on the valve is always the direction of normal water flow.

A pressure switch connected to the 1-inch Tee of the pressure tank is set to turn the pump on at a preset lower pressure limit. It also shuts off the pump at a preset upper pressure limit. A pressure relief valve preset to 75 psi is also connected to the 1-inch Tee of the pressure tank as well as a 0–100 psi gauge to monitor the water pressure at any time. A boiler drain is also connected to the Tee at the bottom of the pressure tank to drain the tank for service.

A main valve is attached to the ¾-inch water line on the house side of the 1-inch Tee of the pressure tank to stop the flow of water from the pressure tank to the house. This ¾-inch line is connected to a Tee above the cold-water connection of the water heater.

The pressure of the house water line will vary, using an on-lot well system between a maximum of 40 and 50 psi. This maximum pressure is preset by using either a 20–40-psi or a 30–50-psi pressure switch at the Tee of the pressure tank. The lower numbers of each psi range are the cut-on pressure for the pump. The pressure relief valve at the Tee of the pressure tank and the temperature pressure relief valve are both preset at 75 psi.

Main valve for cutting off water to the house.

Well System

INLINE WATER FILTERS

SKILL LEVEL

- **Semiskilled**

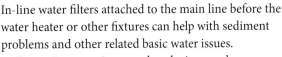

TOOLS REQUIRED

- **Filter housing wrench**
- **Small bucket**
- **Paper towels**

MATERIALS REQUIRED

- **Correct inline filter**
- **Small jug of clean water**

In-line water filters attached to the main line before the water heater or other fixtures can help with sediment problems and other related basic water issues.

For major water issues, other devices, such as an ultraviolet light, water softener, or other major treatment, may also be installed. For best results, determine if the property owner has a maintenance agreement with a plumbing contractor. If not, discuss with him or her the purchase of the correct size and style of filter needed before beginning this task.

The manufacturer and model number of the filter cartridge should be printed on the housing. If not, you may need to take the old one to the home-supply center to obtain a matching filter. Be sure to transport the existing filter in a plastic bag to avoid water leaks. Always fill a gallon jug of water before turning off the main water valve so you have clean water to rinse the cartridge body after removing the used filter.

1 To change the inline water filter, locate the main water supply valve and turn it off. Open a cold water faucet on a level above the inline filter location, such as a kitchen sink, and one below the inline filter location, such as the laundry tub.

2 When the water flowing through the faucets stops, place a bucket under the filter cartridge housing and press and hold the red relief button to relieve any final water pressure inside the cartridge.

Chapter 10 | Water Service

3 After the water stops flowing from the relief button, place the cartridge wrench over the bottom of the cartridge with one hand, apply back pressure to the pipe going into the cartridge, and loosen the cartridge body of the filter in a counterclockwise motion.

4 Place a bucket under the cartridge body and unscrew the cartridge by hand until it disengages from the upper threaded filter housing.

5 Remove the used filter from the cartridge and observe any differences from the previous filter changes. Discard the filter in the trash. Using the gallon jug that you previously filled with water, rinse the cartridge housing thoroughly over a sink before installing the new filter. Note: Make sure that the new filter seats correctly into the bottom of the cartridge housing.

6 Place the cartridge up against the bottom of the upper threaded filter housing that is attached to the main line. Rotate the cartridge counterclockwise until the treads click. This will prevent cross-threading, which is a guaranteed leak problem. Turn the cartridge clockwise by hand to tighten. Place the cartridge wrench over the bottom of the cartridge with one hand. Support the main water pipe connected to the cartridge and snug the cartridge tight in a clockwise direction. Close both faucets on the two levels that allowed the cold water line to drain by gravity at the start. Slowly turn on the house main line valve. You will hear water filling the drained pipes and slowly turn the valve to the full-on position. Check the filter cartridge body for leaks. If leaks occur, turn the main water valve to the off position. Tighten the cartridge more with the wrench with one hand while supporting the main water line connected to the cartridge with the other. Wipe leaks with the paper towels to distinguish them from subsequent leaks. Turn the main water valve back on.

BASIC PLUMBING

PLUMBING REPAIRS

Plumbing repairs are very complex, as they require many distinct parts and materials. In addition, there are many sizes and variations to which these parts must be adapted to fit household fixtures from different periods in time.

Fixtures such as sinks, toilets, showers, and tubs, for example, can span a period of more than seventy years. In that time span, fixtures were made of varied materials, with different types of water and drain connections, and with different finishes. Each fixture will have a different amount of service life left until the next problem occurs or it needs to be replaced completely.

Understanding basic plumbing will go a long way toward understanding what may go wrong with a fixture and the repairs available today to remedy the problem. This includes fixtures, faucets, shut-off valves, riser tubes, and drain parts outside of the finished wall and ceiling surfaces.

The following instructions, illustrations, and tips are meant to guide you through the process of each repair. Also, the skill levels indicated for each repair are meant to keep you from getting in over your head.

Keep the basic plumbing rules in mind:
- Hot is on the left (when facing the faucet).
- Water flows downhill.
- Fixtures will always leak when you least expect them to.

These are just a few. There are others that probably can't be mentioned here!

This book is *not* intended to be a guide for construction, remodeling, or major repair to the house's plumbing system. In most cases, these larger projects would require a licensed, insured plumber to obtain the proper permits and inspections of the completed work.

Tools of the plumbing trade vary greatly. The most common ones used for everyday repairs are illustrated here; you can purchase them at home-supply centers economically.

To purchase these tools in good used condition, visit your local flea market or antique shop or search online at the many sites used to sell personal items. Be sure any used tool purchased is in safe operating condition. Too many injuries and accidents occur because people use tools that should have been discarded. You can also damage your project if a tool slips because it has outlived its useful life!

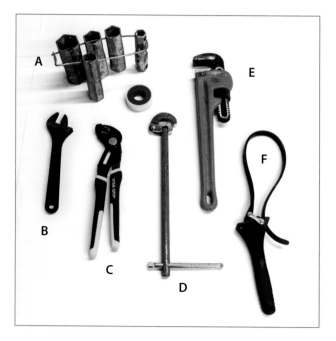

(top left to bottom right)
- **A - faucet nut hex wrenches**
- **B - adjustable wrench**
- **C - groove lock pliers**
- **D - basin; swivel wrench**
- **E - pipe wrench**
- **F - strap wrench**

WATER VALVE CONNECTIONS

SKILL LEVEL

- Semiskilled

TOOLS REQUIRED

- Adjustable wrenches

MATERIAL REQUIRED

- CPVC primer
- CPVC cement
- Teflon™ tape

Many older homes do not include water valve stop connections at the individual fixtures, such as sinks, toilets, or tub/shower units. This was in part due to the acceptable practice at the time and in part because during those early years, most people did not attempt to fix issues.

Today, there is a host of available resources online and in print—such as this book!—to help people achieve successful repairs. Someone told me that online videos have to be under 3 minutes to be viewed as successful. The instructions in this book for tasks take longer than 3 minutes, but who's counting!

The most common types of water valve stop connections are illustrated here. These do not include soldered valve joints, as they are more complicated. Also pictured are the various styles of escutcheon rings that fit over the pipes before any valve stop parts. These hide the rough-in holes in the wall or the floor to provide that finished look.

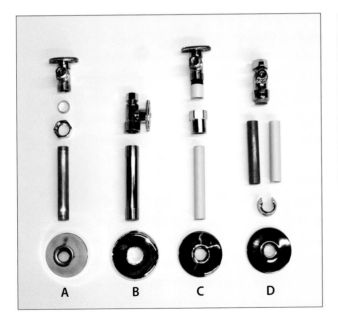

Water valve assembly types

(left to right)

A - **copper pipe**

B - **chrome pipe threaded**

C - **CPVC pipe glued**

D - **copper or PVC pipes with Quick-Connect.**

COPPER PIPE WITH COMPRESSION VALVE STOP

1 Assemble the chrome ½-inch compression nut and then the brass compression ring over the end of the cut copper pipe. Place the valve stop end over the pipe and tighten the hex nut to the valve stop by hand.

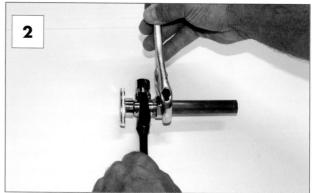

2 Threaded connections can become cross-threaded. Rotate the nut counterclockwise until you hear a click, and then rotate clockwise and tighten by hand. Use two adjustable wrenches facing in opposite directions. With one over the flats of the valve body, and the other over the chrome hex nut, tighten the hex nut in a clockwise direction.

CAUTION

Do not overtighten the hex nut. This can distort the brass compression ring.

CHROME PIPE MALE THREAD WITH FEMALE THREADED VALVE STOP

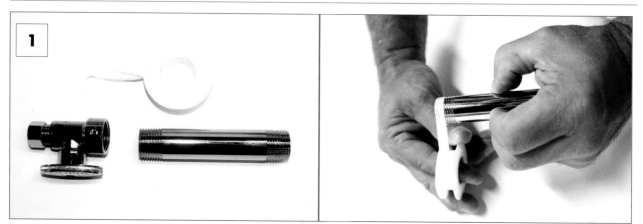

1 For threaded joints, apply Teflon tape to the male thread half of the joint before assembly. Starting at the end of the threads, wrap the Teflon from the roll onto the threads for up to two full wraps. Caution: Be sure to wrap in a clockwise direction when looking at the end of the threads; otherwise, the tape will not seal the threaded joint.

CPVC PLASTIC PIPE WITH MALE THREADED VALVE STOP WITH GLUE ADAPTER

1 Apply primer to both the end of the ½-inch CPVC pipe and the socket of the CPVC valve adapter fitting.

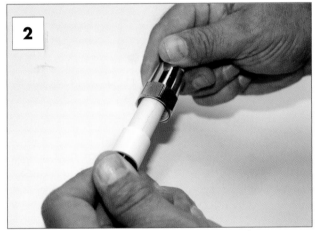

2 Assemble the chrome hex nut over the end of the CPVC pipe. Glue the end of the pipe and the socket of the CPVC valve adapter fitting, and join them with a quarter turn. Hold together with pressure until the glue sets.

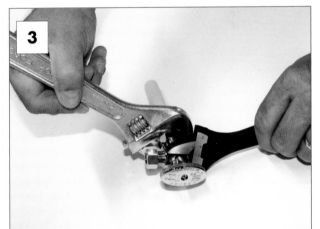

3 Attach the valve stop to the chrome hex nut and tighten by hand. Apply an additional quarter turn with the two adjustable wrenches thirty minutes after gluing.

COPPER AND CPVC PIPE WITH QUICK-CONNECT VALVE STOPS

Quick-Connect valve stops are intended to save time. However, they are more expensive than the previously discussed conventional valve stops. In addition to the valve stop, you must purchase a quick disconnect ring tool specific from the manufacturer of the valve stop.

Chapter 11 | Basic Plumbing

WATER LINES AND HOSES

Valve stops must be connected to the fixture using a water line. In the past, this was a ⅜-inch chrome pipe that was bent to conform to create a finished appearance between the valve stop and the fixture. Today, we use flexible stainless-steel hose connections for a leakproof connection to eliminate the need to establish offset bends for a riser tube.

The most common types of ⅜-inch stainless-steel hose and PVC lines are illustrated here.

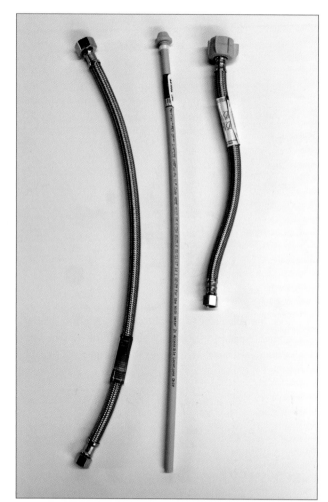

(left to right) Faucet; faucet (CPVC); toilet.

When you use the ⅜-inch stainless-steel hose, you do not use the ⅜-inch chrome compression nut and brass compression ring that are included with the valve stop. The stainless-steel hose for faucets and toilets have that ⅜-inch compression nut and flare included on one end.

When using a ⅜-inch CPVC or chrome metal riser tube, use the ⅜-inch compression nut and brass compression ring from the valve stop. Note: When reused, ⅜-inch brass compression rings may not reseal the ⅜-inch riser. These are available separately at home-supply centers in the plumbing section.

CAUTION

Take care to expose enough pipe to seat into the Quick-Connect valve stop.

CHAPTER 12

KITCHEN PLUMBING REPAIRS

KITCHEN FAUCET

Chapter 12 | Kitchen Plumbing Repairs

Kitchen faucet repairs can include handle replacements, individual water valve stem connections, hose sprayers, faucet cartridges, or entire faucets. With a faucet, it depends on its age, model, and manufacturer whether every service part will be available. If the faucet is very old or obsolete, or the manufacturer is no longer in business, then you may need a complete faucet replacement. After determining whether you need a repair or a replacement, obtain the correct parts or faucet before you begin your work.

Complete Faucet Replacement

Turn off the valve stop for the hot and cold water under the sink. If you are not sure whether they work properly or if they do not exist, then turn the main water supply valve off for the whole house. Clear out any items from the cabinet under the sink so you have plenty of room to work. Secure a flashlight and small bucket to catch any water that drips from the faucet supply tubes.

Using an adjustable wrench or faucet wrench, unscrew the nuts securing the riser tubes to the faucet. If the existing faucet has a spray hose attachment, unscrew that connection. Also unscrew the nut that secures that hose escutcheon and remove that.

Remove the riser tubes from the valve stops and set them aside. Using an adjustable wrench, faucet wrench, or faucet socket, unscrew the faucet deck nuts. It's a clever idea to have someone standing at the sink to help keep the faucet from falling into the sink bowl and causing damage while you're working under the sink.

After you've removed all of the parts from the faucet mounting deck, clean the area to accept the new faucet and spray nozzle escutcheon. Make a complete list of parts needed to complete the faucet replacement, including new riser tubes, Teflon tape, plumber's putty, and clear silicone-latex caulk.

Take a picture of the faucet mounting deck or take the existing faucet to the home-supply center to best match the mounting profile and number of holes used. If the new faucet uses fewer holes than the original one, you have a few options.

1. Purchase a chrome-plated snap-in round cover plate to close the unused hole.
2. Purchase a deck-mounted soap dispenser to use in the unused hole.
3. Purchase a deck-mounted water filter dispenser spout to use in the unused hole.

Unpack the new faucet parts and make sure everything is there before starting the replacement. Dry-fit the faucet and accessory parts in the holes of the mounting deck. Make sure that the hole openings will be covered by the new parts and that you are satisfied with the look and style before proceeding. Follow the specific manufacturer's instructions, including the method of sealing the new faucet to the existing mounting deck.

Have someone hold the faucet in the correct position as you install and tighten the faucet mounting nuts on the underside of the sink. Continue with any replacement accessories and tighten them from the underside of the sink. Connect the new riser tubes to the existing connections for the valve stops or other existing methods. Turn on the main water-supply valve if you had turned it off previously.

Place dry paper towels under the sink inside the cabinet to detect any water leaks. Slowly open one valve stop at a time to check for water leaks on the dry paper towels between the valve stop and the faucet first. Next, slowly open the faucet to allow only cold water to flow to check the faucet for leaks. Then, open the faucet to allow only hot water to flow to check the faucet for leaks. If there are no leaks, the faucet replacement was a success. Congratulations!

Faucet Handle or Knob Replacement

If your existing faucet is still in production or is supported by replacement parts, you are in luck.

To replace the handle or knob(s) of a faucet, you must locate the screw that attaches the handle or knob(s) to the valve stem. Many times, it is under a chrome trim cap or under caps labeled "H" and "C" (for knobs). Many times, an Internet search will display the assembly diagram of the product you have. Remove the cap covering the attachment screw and unscrew the handle or knob(s).

Remove the handle or knob(s) and take it along to the home-supply center to compare to the new replacement parts. Note: Using the Internet to search for common parts is also a helpful means of obtaining the correct parts if they are not available locally.

Reinstall the handle or the knob(s) and check their operation to be sure they do not become loose or bind in any way when turning them on or off.

Hot- and Cold-Water Valve-Stem Replacement

Turn off the valve stops below the sink or the main house valve. Use the methods above in handle and knob(s) replacement. Remove the existing handle or knob(s). Remove the stem escutcheon. Remove the valve stem nut that secure it into the faucet base. Use a faucet socket, socket, and ratchet or adjustable wrench. Remove the valve stem by rotating it to unscrew it from the faucet deck. Be sure to remove the sealing parts with the old valve stem.

Install the new valve stem replacements by screwing them back into the faucet deck. Be sure to install the new sealing parts with the new valve stems. Install the valve-stem nut and tighten securely. Install the valve-stem escutcheons, handles, or knob(s). Tighten the handle or knob screws and install the caps over the screws. Turn on the valve stops below the sink or the main house valve.

Slowly open the cold-water side of the faucet and check for leaks. Slowly open the hot-water side of the faucet

and check for leaks. If there are no leaks, the valve-stem replacement was successful. Congratulations!

Valve Body Cartridge Replacement

If your existing faucet is still in production or is supported by replacement parts, you are in luck. Turn off the valve stops below the sink or the main house valve. Use the methods above in handle and knob(s) replacement.

Remove the existing handle or knob(s). Remove the escutcheon trim nut by using a strap wrench or other method that will not scratch the finish. Remove the stem escutcheon. Remove the valve body cartridge by removing the retaining ring at the top of the cartridge. Slightly pry under the top of the cartridge to start. It is held in place by O-rings that seal the cartridge to the faucet valve body.

Install the new valve body cartridge by carefully aligning the cartridge with the valve body opening. Many cartridges have a slot and keyway in the faucet to prevent incorrect installation. Gently push the cartridge straight down. Be sure not to damage the cartridge or the O-rings that seal the cartridge in the valve body opening. Install the retaining ring over the cartridge. Install the cartridge escutcheon and the escutcheon nut securely, using a strap wrench or another tool that will not damage the finish. Install the handles or knob(s). Tighten handle or knob screws and install the caps over the screws. Turn on the valve stops below the sink or the main house valve that was turned off.

Slowly open the cold-water side of the faucet and check for leaks. Slowly open the hot-water side of the faucet and check for leaks. If the faucet doesn't work properly, you may have installed the cartridge backward or otherwise incorrectly. If there are no leaks, the valve body cartridge works correctly, and your replacement was successful. Congratulations!

Chapter 12 | Kitchen Plumbing Repairs

KITCHEN SINK STRAINER BASKET

SKILL LEVEL

- Semiskilled

TOOLS REQUIRED

- Groove lock pliers
- Small bucket

MATERIALS NEEDED

- New strainer basket kit
- Plumber's putty
- Teflon™ tape
- Paper towels

A kitchen sink will have a strainer bowl and a basket for each bowl. The finish of the strainer bowl and basket will match that of the sink. The purpose of a strainer basket kit in a kitchen sink is to adapt the opening that was made to fit with the proper drain connections. If a garbage disposal is used in one of the drain locations, then you will not need a strainer basket kit for that drain location.

1 The strainer basket kit includes a snap-in drain basket, a strainer bowl, rubber and paper washers for under the sink, a mounting cup, a hex retaining nut, and a plastic washer for the tailpiece and attachment nut. Unpack the new parts, completely read the manufacturer's instructions, and be sure all of the parts are included.

2 Turn off the water to the faucet at the valve stops under the sink. If the valve stop does not stop the flow of water from the faucet, locate and turn off the house main water valve.

3 Remove the existing P-trap under the kitchen sink. Follow the instructions in the Kitchen Sink Drain P-Trap repair section (page 118). Using groove lock pliers, hold the tailpiece with one hand and loosen and remove the nut securing the tailpiece that is connected to the strainer basket's drain cup.

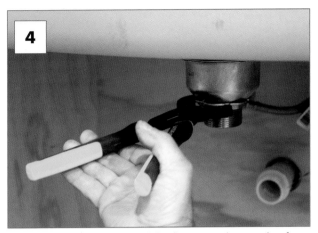

4 Remove the tailpiece and the flange washer inside of it. Use the groove lock pliers to loosen and remove the hex nut securing the mounting cup.

5 Remove the mounting cup, paper washer, and rubber washer from underside of the strainer bowl.

6 Remove the existing strainer bowl from the top side of the sink. Remove any existing plumber's putty that remains in the drain's recessed area. Place plumber's putty under the flange of the new strainer bowl to create a watertight seal in the recessed area of the sink drain opening. Put the putty between your palms, roll it into a thick string, and then place the rolled putty around the underside of the flange.

Chapter 12 | Kitchen Plumbing Repairs

7 From the sink side, install the strainer bowl into the sink drain opening. Be sure that the flange is flat and centered in the recess. Allow a small amount of plumber's putty to squeeze out from under the flange. Note: At this point, it is helpful if a second person keeps downward pressure on the flange while you attach the parts to the strainer basket bowl.

8 From the underside of the sink, install the rubber and paper washers and the mounting cup, in that order. While holding the parts from the previous step with one hand, start to thread the hex retaining nut onto the threaded end of the strainer bowl and snug by hand.

✓ TIP

At this time, be sure that the flange on the sink side of the strainer bowl is still flat and centered in the drain recess area.

9 Using groove lock pliers, tighten the retaining hex nut completely. This will allow more of the plumber's putty to squeeze out from under the strainer bowl flange inside the sink. Clean the remaining amount of plumber's putty from around the flange in the sink for a professionally finished look.

10 Apply Teflon tape to the threaded end of the strainer bowl using two complete wraps per revolution. Note: Be sure to wrap the tape in a clockwise rotation, looking at the end of the threads. This will prevent the tape from unwinding itself when you tighten the tailpiece hex nut.

11 Place the new flange washer seal into the end of the vertical tailpiece and attach it to the end of the threaded strainer bowl.

12 Using groove lock pliers, tighten the hex nut snugly to create a watertight seal. Reinstall the 1½-inch P-trap following the instructions in the Kitchen Sink Drain P-Trap repair section (page 118). Turn the valve stop or the main house valve back on. Place a paper towel under the sink on the shelf. Run cold water first to check the joints of the vertical tailpiece and P-trap. If leaks occur, tighten the compression nuts. Wipe up leaks with a paper towel to distinguish subsequent leaks. Run the hot water next to check for any further leaks.

Place a bucket under the assembled P-trap drain assembly in case there are any leaks when you test the plumber's putty and rubber washer that seals the strainer bowl and the sink drain opening. Place the drain basket into the strainer bowl until you hear a click. Run the hot water until there are a few inches of water in the sink. Allow the water to stand for a short period of time. Check the rubber washer on the underside of the sink for leaks. If leaks occur, retighten the retaining hex nut of the strainer cup. Wipe up any leaks with a paper towel to distinguish subsequent leaks. Note: I leave the empty bucket under the sink for a period of time. This gives a good indication if the connections are sealed properly. It also protects the bottom shelf of the cabinet from water damage. If the bucket stays empty and dry, you have successfully completed this repair!

Kitchen Sink Strainer Basket

KITCHEN SINK DRAIN P-TRAP

SKILL LEVEL

- Semiskilled

TOOLS REQUIRED

- Groove lock pliers
- Small bucket

MATERIALS REQUIRED

- New 1½-inch P-trap kit

Kitchen sink drain repairs cover several key parts that must work efficiently and correctly so that sink water flows into the drain system and not into the cabinet under your sink.

✓ TIP

The parts shown here are sold as complete replacement kits or separate parts at home-supply centers. Be sure to take the defective part with you because P-traps come in two different sizes. You will need to purchase parts for a 1½-inch kitchen sink drain.

1½-INCH P-TRAP REPLACEMENT

The drain in your kitchen sink will clog over time from food, soap scum, and the occasional object that falls into the sink and—*swoosh*—down the drain it goes. The drain's inside diameter becomes smaller and smaller as more food, hair, and soap scum build up slowly.

Advertisements will lead you to believe that your drain can be unclogged magically if you purchase a certain type of drain cleaner. Don't get me wrong—sometimes it works, but, many times, the first, second, or third bottle may *not* do the trick.

The P-trap for a kitchen sink can be either chrome-plated brass or PVC. The PVC type is preferred if the property is known to have hard water.

The easiest and foolproof way to clean the P-trap for a kitchen sink is to disassemble the trap completely. This way, you will be able to see where the clog is and how much buildup is inside the trap. Turn off the water to the sink underneath at the valve stop. If the valve does not stop the flow of water from the faucet, locate and shut off the main house valve.

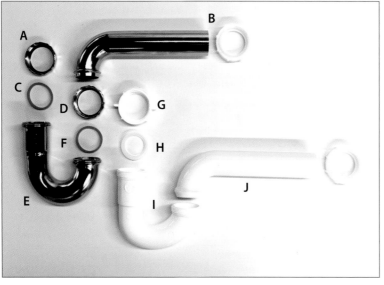

1½-inch chrome P-trap parts

A - chrome compression nut

B - chrome 7-inch wall tube with trap adapter nut

C - red rubber washer

D - chrome compression nut

E - chrome J-bend

F - red rubber washer

1½-inch PVC P-trap parts

G - PVC compression nut

H - plastic compression washer

I - PVC J-bend

J - PVC 7-inch wall tube with trap adapter nut

1 Loosen the compression nut between the J-bend of the trap and the vertical tailpiece. Place a small bucket under the P-trap to catch any water from the vertical tailpiece and J-bend. Loosen the compression nut between the back of the J-bend and 7-inch wall tube. Allow the J-bend to drop into the bucket.

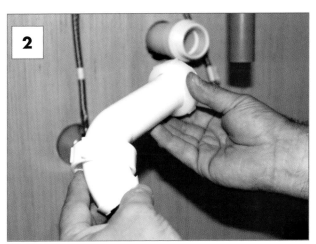

2 Loosen the trap adapter compression nut and remove the 7-inch wall tube.

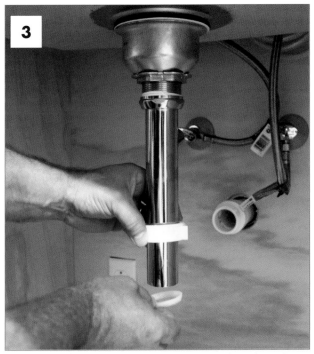

3 Also remove the compression washer and nut from the vertical tailpiece. After you've removed all of the P-trap pieces, take them to a utility sink or to an outdoor hose and clean the inside of the trap parts to get rid of any buildup. Also check the compression washer that seals the top of the J-bend to the tailpiece. If this is worn out, replace it with a new one.

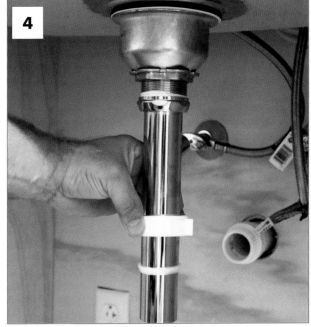

4 Re-install the cleaned P-trap 7-inch wall tube with the compression nut over the open end of the pipe that is inserted into the trap adapter. Tighten the compression nut by hand. Insert the compression nut and compression washer over the bottom of the vertical tailpiece. Insert the top of the J-bend over the tailpiece with the compression nut and ring already in place.

Chapter 12 | Kitchen Plumbing Repairs

5 Align the bottom of the J-bend with the end of the 7-inch wall piece and start the threaded connections by hand. Align the threads of all of the joints. To prevent cross-threading the compression nuts, rotate the nut counterclockwise until you hear a click. Rotate the compression nut clockwise and hand-tighten it snugly.

Place a paper towel under the reinstalled P-trap. Turn on the hot and cold valve stops or the main water valve. Run cold water first, and then the hot water, to check for leaks.

CHROME METAL P-TRAPS

For chrome metal P-traps, the instructions are the same. The washer between the J-bend and 7-inch wall tube pipe is a flat rubber washer. The washer at the top of the J-bend over the tailpiece can be a flat rubber or plastic tapered washer as shown.

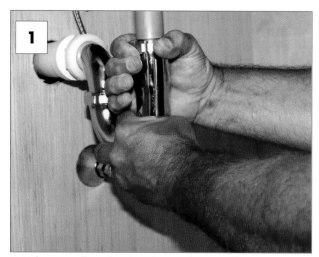

1 When installing the chrome metal P-trap, the compression nut threads can become cross-threaded. Be sure to align the threads by rotating the nut backward until you hear a click and then rotating the nut clockwise and tightening by hand.

2 Compression nuts for chrome metal P-traps require groove lock pliers to tighten the nuts completely after hand-tightening.

CAUTION

Do not over tighten. Use the tool for only a half or three-quarter turn beyond hand-tight.

Kitchen Sink Drain P-Trap

GARBAGE DISPOSAL

SKILL LEVEL

- Skilled

TOOLS REQUIRED

- Four-way screwdriver
- Manufacturer's hex key wrench
- Small bucket
- Hammer

MATERIALS REQUIRED

- New disposal unit
- Plumber's putty
- New cord set (if applicable)

Electric garbage disposal.

Electric garbage disposals are a great modern convenience for discarding unwanted table scraps. These units also play a key role in the draining of electric dishwashers. Any food particles that drain from your dishwasher into your disposal will sink to the bottom of the disposal and be ground the next time you turn on the switch to activate the disposal.

Before adding a disposal to the house's plumbing system, check with the property owner. On-lot septic systems *may not* be deemed compatible with the use of disposals.

Troubleshooting and Maintenance

The sink garbage disposal has a built-in overload circuit that will automatically open if the disposal becomes lodged with solid materials, such as food, bones, or silverware. If the disposal stops working, first check to see if the red circuit-overload button is activated; if so, it will be sticking out of the bottom of the disposal. Make sure to turn the power switch off and use a flashlight to see if any foreign matter is lodged in the disposal. **Do not place your hands in a disposal connected to the plumbing or electrical systems.**

1 If you find something lodged in the disposal, you must unplug the power cord for safety before attempting to dislodge the material. Use the hex wrench that is supplied with the disposal. Insert the wrench into the bottom hex hole of the disposal. Turn the wrench in a counterclockwise motion first, and then reverse the motion to clockwise to dislodge the material. Plug the unit back into the wall receptacle and push the red circuit-overload button back in. Open the sink faucet cold-water line and allow water to run down the disposal drain. With the water running, turn on the switch to see if the disposal operates. Listen for odd

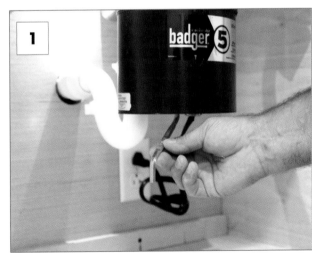

noises that were not apparent when the disposal previously operated correctly. If everything is back to normal, drop a few ice cubes down the disposal drain and run the water until the ice is completely chopped. This helps lubricate and sharpen the disposal blades.

Chapter 12 | Kitchen Plumbing Repairs

2 If the material doesn't become dislodged, the best remedy is to completely remove the unit from the bottom of the sink and place it on a towel on the countertop. To accomplish this, unplug the disposal from the wall receptacle. Place a small empty bucket under the J-bend of the P-trap and loosen and remove the compression nuts that seal the trap joints. Reach under the sink where the quick-disconnect ring attaches the disposal to the disposal sink strainer. Twist the locking ring counterclockwise to disconnect the disposal. Be careful, as the disposal has weight to it. Note: Once you've disconnected the disposal from the electric and plumbing systems, it is safe to stick your hand and/or tools into the disposal opening to dislodge any matter that the hex wrench wouldn't by turning the motor shaft.

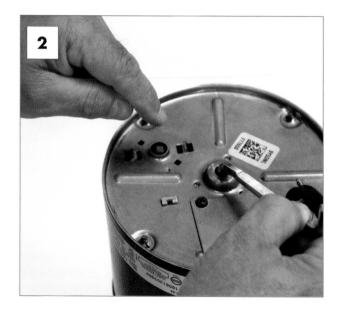

REPLACEMENT AND INSTALLATION

When you need to completely replace your disposal or install a new disposal, the new unit must be the correct size. Disposals are rated by motor horsepower. The higher the horsepower, the stronger the disposal is. Most homes can rely on the dependability of a ⅓- or ½-horsepower unit. Note: Be sure to read and follow all of the instructions and be sure to register the disposal unit for the factory warranty.

Manufacturers of disposal units usually *do not* include the flexible power cord with the three-prong plug. You can purchase this kit separately from the home-supply center. If you are replacing your disposal, you can use the original flexible cord if it is in good working order.

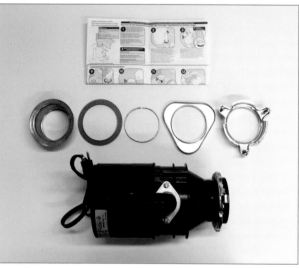

Disposal and mounting parts.

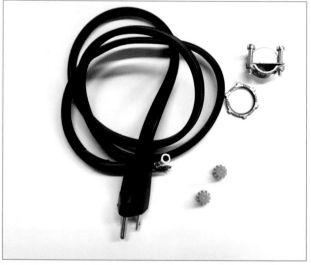

The flexible power cord with three-prong plug is usually not included with disposal units and must be purchased separately.

1 Loosen the screw that attaches the wire access door and insert a ⅜–inch metal cable connector into the hole with the flat locking nut on the inside of the wire access opening.

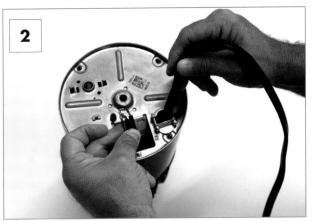

2 Tighten the nut and connector completely. Feed the stripped wire end of the flexible power cable into the cable connector and feed out through the cable access opening.

3 Attach the ground screw connector to the green ground screw and tighten securely.

4 Connect the black wire of the disposal unit to one of the black stripped wires of the flexible power cable. Secure with the orange wire nut supplied. Next, connect the white wire of the disposal unit to the remaining black stripped wire of the flexible power cable. Secure with the orange wire nut supplied.

5 Tighten the two cable connector strain-relief screws with a screwdriver to secure the flexible power cable.

✓TIP

This prevents the cable from being pulled out of the cable connector and causing electrical shorts, poor electrical connections, or shock hazards.

Chapter 12 | Kitchen Plumbing Repairs

6 Reinstall the wire access opening door and tighten by hand with a screwdriver.

7 For new unit replacement with a dishwasher that drains into the disposal first before the water continues into the drain system, use a flat-head screwdriver to "knock out" the molded disk in the dishwasher's hose drain inlet. Note: If you do not have a dishwasher that drains into the disposal, then skip this step. Keeping the molded disc in place prevents the disposal from leaking when the disposal overflows.

8 For the new disposal, you will need to attach the drain elbow to the drain outlet port of the disposal. First, locate the round rubber washer gasket and place it in the recessed area of the drain outlet port.

9 Next, insert the metal attachment flange over the straight open end of the disposal drain elbow and slide it up to the collar of the disposal drain elbow.

10 Locate the two attachment flange screws, insert into the threaded holes, and tighten by hand with a screwdriver to create a leakproof seal between the disposal elbow and the drain outlet port.

Chapter 12 | Kitchen Plumbing Repairs

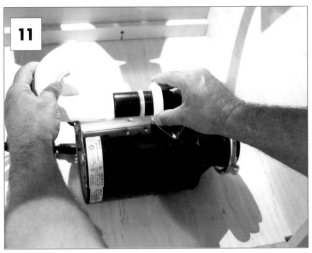

11 Install the J-bend compression nut and compression washer and tighten by hand onto the J-bend of the P-trap.

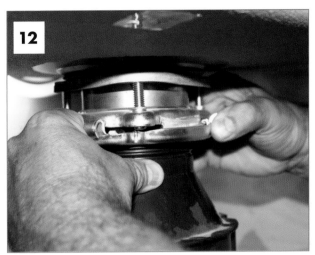

12 Reattach the disposal's quick-disconnect collar to the existing sink strainer and rotate the connection collar of the disposal clockwise to secure and seal.

To check the newly installed disposal unit, drain elbow, and P-trap assembly, place a dry paper towel on the shelf of the sink cabinet. Run cold water first to check for leaks at all connections. If no leaks occur, run hot water to check for leaks at all connections. If leaks are evident, retighten the joint connections to be sure they are correct.

> **✓ TIP**
>
> Wipe up water from any leaks before retesting. This prevents previous leaks from being confused with any new leaks.

REPAIRING, REMOVING, AND REPLACING DISPOSAL SINK STRAINER

The disposal sink strainer requires a complete seal between the bottom of the strainer flange and the sink's drain opening. Sometimes this seal becomes degraded because the weight of the disposal hanging from it under the sink causes it to leak. When installing a new sink disposal, it may be of a different manufacturer or model, so the quick-disconnect flange may not be compatible.

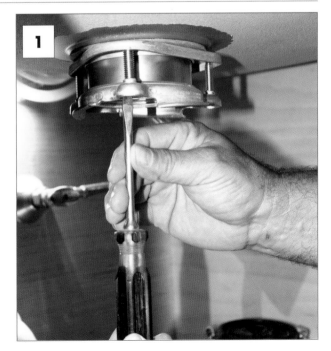

1 To remove the existing disposal's Quick-Connect mount flange, loosen the three screws that apply pressure between the top and bottom mounting plates.

Chapter 12 | Kitchen Plumbing Repairs

2 Raise the lower mounting plate to expose the snap ring that retains the bottom mounting plate and pry on the ring with a flat-head screwdriver.

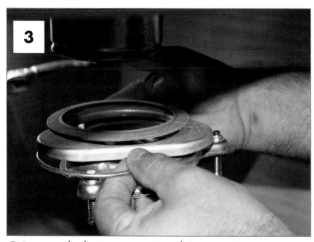

3 Remove the bottom mounting plate, snap ring, top mounting plate, and gasket that seals the bottom of the sink's drain opening.

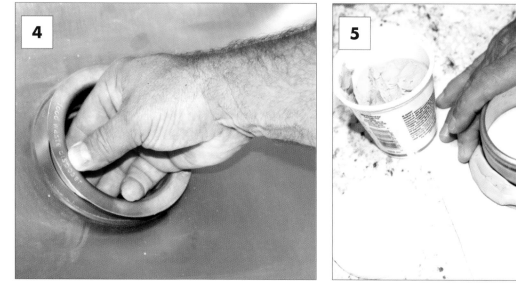

4 Now you can remove the disposal strainer from the sink's drain opening and clean any plumber's putty residue left on the drain hole's recessed area.

5 Remove some plumber's putty from the container and roll it between your fingers to create a string of putty. With the disposal strainer turned over, place the string of putty around the flange as shown.

Chapter 12 | Kitchen Plumbing Repairs

6 Pick up the disposal strainer by the end with the retainer ring groove with one hand, grab the flange's outside edge with the other, and carefully align the disposal strainer with the drain opening and insert it into the hole. Apply light, even pressure around the flange to seat the putty.

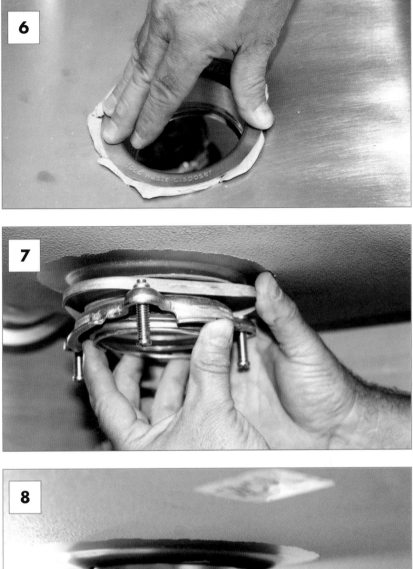

7 From the underside of the sink, install the gasket that seals the bottom of the sink over the end of the disposal strainer. Keep pressure on the gasket to prevent it from sliding off the disposal strainer. Next, install the top mounting plate, bottom mounting plate, and snap ring. Be sure that the snap ring clicks into the snap-ring groove.

8 Tighten by hand the three screws from the bottom mounting plate until they make contact with the top mounting plate under the sink. Then, tighten all three screws completely with a screwdriver to apply the correct pressure between the underside of the sink and the disposal strainer flange.

Chapter 12 | Kitchen Plumbing Repairs

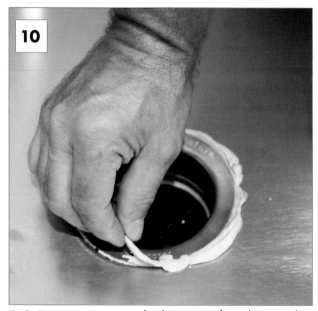

10 Remove any excess plumber's putty from the top side of the disposal strainer flange in the sink.

9 From under the sink, raise and attach the disposal to the quick-mount flange and tighten the disposal ring by hand. Note: Reconnect the drain hose to the dishwasher if one exists. Connect the J-bend of the trap to the 7-inch wall tube that exits the trap adapter fitting at the wall of the cabinet. Tighten all of the compression nuts completely by hand to create a tight, leakproof drain assembly.

You must check the disposal strainer flange and the sink opening seal for leaks before using the disposal. Place the disposal drain plug into the disposal strainer. Run hot water into the sink to fill the sink with a few inches of water. Place paper towels on the cabinet shelf under the disposal. If the seal leaks where you installed the plumber's putty, you will see wet spots on the paper towels. If leaks occur at this point, further tighten the three screws at the bottom mounting plates of the disposal to apply more pressure between the underside of the sink and disposal strainer flange.

✓ **TIP**

Use new paper towels for each leak test, including that of the P-trap's compression nut joints.

Chapter 12 | Kitchen Plumbing Repairs

CHAPTER 13

BATHROOMS

BATHROOM ACCESSORIES

SKILL LEVEL

- Basic

TOOLS REQUIRED

- Pencil
- Small flat-head screwdriver
- Tape measure
- Cordless drill
- ¼- inch drill bit
- 2-foot level

MATERIALS REQUIRED

- As supplied by manufacturer

Bathroom accessories are essential to any bathroom. The more people using a bathroom, the more towel bars and towel rings you will need to keep the bathroom orderly.

Towel bars are usually mounted at two standard heights: 48 inches and 66 inches above the floor. The length of towel bars varies widely. The most common length is 24 inches; however, they are available in 6-inch increments up to 36 inches. They are made of various materials and come in different finishes.

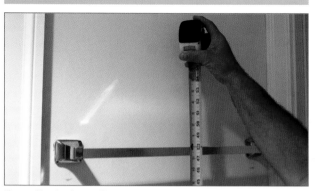
The usual height of a towel bar.

Towel bars installed along a wall are generally mounted at 48 inches to the center above the finished floor. If you need a towel bar to be higher than 48 inches from the floor, install it at 66 inches to the center above the finished floor. This elevated height allows you to hang towels above the toilet tank or to hang longer towels along a wall.

Towel rings are usually installed as close to the vanity as possible, often over the vanity surface for easy access and to prevent water drops from getting on the floor and being a slipping hazard. The mounting block of the towel bar is located 66 inches to the center, above the finished floor. Measuring from the vanity top, that would be 36 inches above old-style vanities and 30 inches above new-style vanities. Note: Keep the towel rings/hand towels away from the GFCI receptacles at the vanity location.

Keep towel rings away from GFCI receptacles.

Mount the toilet paper holder close to the toilet. The holder is generally located 24 inches to the center above the finished floor and 32 inches to the center from the back wall of the toilet. Note: The packaging of a bathroom accessory will include an installation template for that item. Read and follow the included instructions and use the mounting hardware included with your item.

The usual height of a toilet paper holder.

BATHROOM EXHAUST FAN AND LIGHT

SKILL LEVEL

- **Basic**

TOOLS REQUIRED

- **Stepladder (Note: Follow stepladder safety precautions)**

MATERIALS REQUIRED

- **Light bulb (maximum 60 watts)**

Maintaining a bathroom fan/light combination only requires replacing the light bulb as needed and cleaning the inlet grill and fan blades.

1 Stand on the stepladder and determine which two sides of the light lens have the tabs that lock the lens into the trim ring against the ceiling. Use your fingertips to apply pressure simultaneously to both of the sides with the locking tabs to disengage them from the slots. Remove the lens and rest it on the vanity countertop.

✓ TIP

It will not require modifications of wiring, ceiling openings or exhaust ducts if the models are the same.

2 With the switch off, remove the nonworking light bulb and replace with a new light bulb of 60 watts or less to prevent overheating that can damage the lens. Clean the fan blades and the inlet grill openings in the ceiling trim. This will help with performance efficiency. Reinstall the lens, with the locking tabs aligned with the slots, and snap into place. Turn the light switch on to check the bulb operation. If more than the light bulb requires attention, identify the make and model of the fan/light combination.

It is possible the unit may still be in production, and, if so, buying a new one will provide the necessary parts to make the unit operate correctly again.

Chapter 13 | Bathrooms

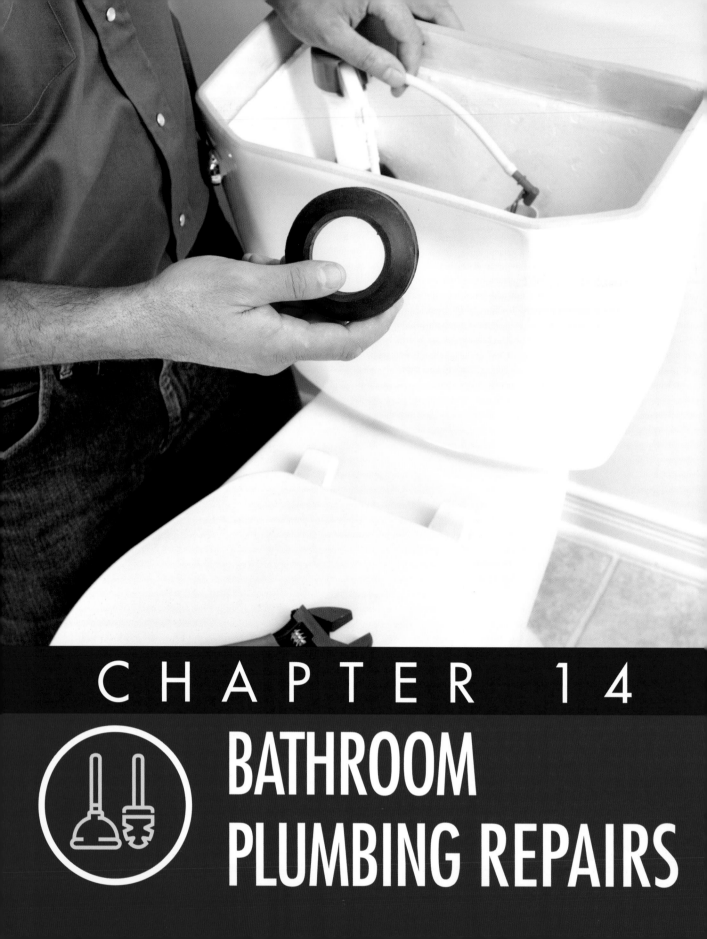

BATHROOM PLUMBING REPAIRS

VANITY FAUCET

SKILL LEVEL

- Semiskilled

TOOLS REQUIRED

- Adjustable wrench

MATERIALS REQUIRED

- New faucet

Bathroom vanity faucets have been produced in many styles, shapes, and finishes. The original two-handle models of the 1940s and 1950s are still in service today. This design was made using flat compression washers to stop the flow of water. Modern faucets made in the 1980s and beyond use a plastic cartridge with an O-ring design to stop the flow of water.

Choose a faucet that will replace the existing one using the same center distance for the hot and cold water lines. For a vanity, this is usually a 4-inch center.

1 Turn off the water at the valve stop under the vanity. If this does *not* stop the flow of water from the faucet, locate and turn off the main house valve. For comfort when working under the vanity, place a folded towel over the bottom cabinet rail. This rail is made from hardwood and has a sharp edge on the outside corner, where you will be lying.

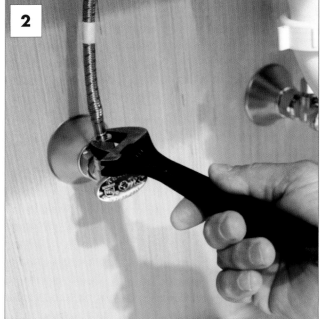

2 Disconnect the faucet riser tubes at the valve stops using an adjustable wrench.

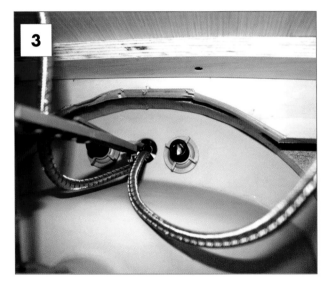

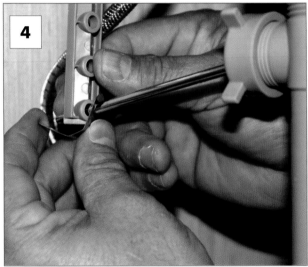

3 Lying on your back, remove the faucet end of the riser tubes with an adjustable wrench as well as the plastic deck-mounting nuts that secure the faucet. Note: For older-style faucets, the deck-mounting nuts will be brass and require an adjustable wrench to loosen them.

4 Remove the metal spring clip from the end of the pop-up drain lever. This will allow you to remove the adjustable vertical bar attached to the pop-up drain handle with the faucet. Note: This can be attached to the new faucet pop-up drain handle before installing the new faucet.

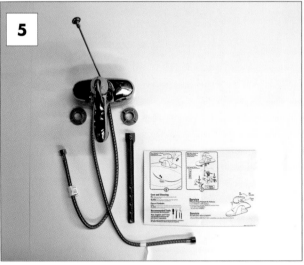

5 Unpack the new faucet and read the instructions. The new faucet will also include a new pop-up drain assembly. Use paper towels to clean the sink's top surface where the existing faucet was mounted. Insert the new faucet into the existing holes, attach the faucet under the sink with the deck-mounting nuts, and tighten by hand.

✓ TIP

If a second person is available to hold the faucet centered in place while you tighten the deck-mounting nuts underneath, it will makes your job a lot easier!

Some faucets are now available with factory-installed water lines at the faucet end. This requires only the ⅜-inch compression nut connection to be made at the valve stop. Reconnect the pop-up drain lever to the adjustable vertical bar by installing the metal spring clip. Note: The pop-up drain plug must be at the maximum height when the drain handle is pushed down completely.

Turn on the water to the faucet by opening the valve stop for the hot and cold water, or turning on the main house valve if you turned it off. Check for leaks at the faucet water lines connected to the hot- and cold-water valve stops. Retighten the ⅜-inch compression nuts if leaks occur. Wipe the leaks dry with paper towels to distinguish subsequent leaks.

VANITY POP-UP

SKILL LEVEL

- **Basic**

TOOLS REQUIRED

- **Groove lock pliers**
- **Small bucket**
- **Paper towels**

MATERIALS REQUIRED

- **Plumber's putty or clear silicone**
- **Teflon™ tape**

The parts that make up the pop-up drain assembly are illustrated here.

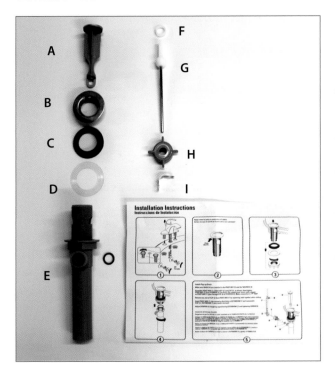

Pop-up drain assemblies are very straightforward in their purpose and use for vanity sinks. By pulling on the drain handle at the faucet, the pop-up will be drawn down into the drain opening and create a seal to stop the flow of water. Pushing the drain handle downward raises the pop-up so the water being held back will flow nicely down the drain.

So, for a feature that works so simply, there are many issues that arise to make these simple pop-ups not so simple—not the least of which is when the pop-up goes missing. It's hard to stop water when no one knows where the pop-up is!

Another issue is the pop-up connects to a lever located inside the drain so it doesn't become loose and goes missing. This lever is the first area that hair and soap scum attach to in the drain system to begin that annoying drain clog.

Just as the pop-up can go missing, so can the pull handle that makes the pop-up go up and down. This happens because somehow the metal screw under the sink that secures the pull handle to the pop-up drain assembly becomes loose, and the handle pulls completely out of the faucet.

Lastly, because of the chemicals in the personal-care products we buy, the seal between the bottom of the chrome drain fitting and the sink's drain hole can deteriorate and create a leak under the sink.

(left side, top to bottom)

- A - **pop-up stopper**
- B - **drain threaded flange**
- C - **under-sink rubber washer**
- D - **plastic washer**
- E - **pop-up drain tube with nut and O-ring**

(right side, top to bottom)

- F - **plastic washer lever**
- G - **pop-up lever**
- H - **compression nut**
- I - **metal spring clip.**

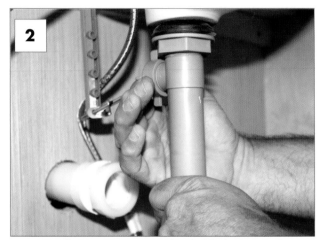

1 To begin servicing or replacing the pop-up drain assembly, it is best to shut the hot and cold water off under the sink. If valve stops are not present, close the main water shut-off valve. This prevents the faucet from being turned on while you are working on the drain. Place a small bucket under the sink's P-trap drain to catch any water that may leak out of the pop-up drain. Locate the metal spring clip that secure the pop-up lever to the adjustment bar. Pinch the metal ends together and slide the clip off the pop-up lever.

2 Loosen the compression nut that holds the pop-up lever and internal plastic seal.

✓ TIP

If the pop-up is being replaced instead of repaired, you may purchase one separately at a home-supply center, or one will be included in a pop-up drain kit that you can purchase.

3 Remove the assembly from the pop-up drain tube.

4 The pop-up drain can be removed from the sink drain. To remove the pop-up drain assembly, you must first remove the P-trap by loosening the compression nuts that seal the joints of the J-bend and 7-inch wall tube. Set these parts aside for further inspection, cleaning, and assembly. See the Vanity Drain P-Trap section (page 139).

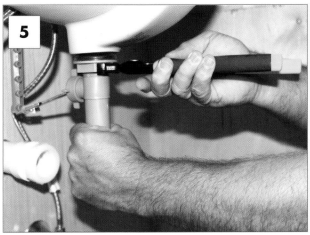

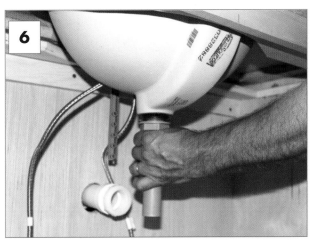

5 To disconnect the pop-up drain tube from the sink drain flange, use groove lock pliers to loosen the hex nut under the sink.

6 Next, grab the pop-up drain tube with one hand and unscrew it from the threaded drain flange.

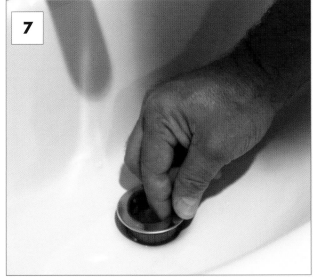

7 From the sink side, remove the chrome threaded sink flange and remove any plumber's putty residue.

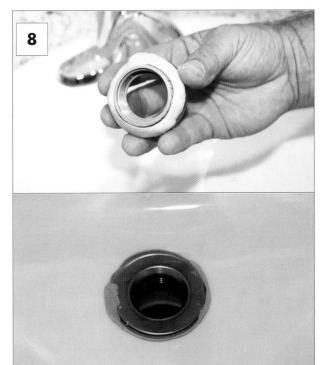

8 Apply new plumber's putty under the chrome threaded sink flange to seal it to the top of the sink drain surface. (You can use clear silicone instead of plumber's putty, especially for cultured marble and solid surface finishes.) Press the drain flange into the sink drain opening. Some newer pop-up drain assemblies have built-in rubber seals, eliminating the need for addition sealing.

Chapter 14 | Bathroom Plumbing Repairs

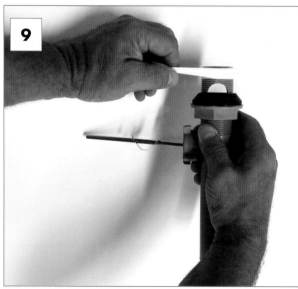

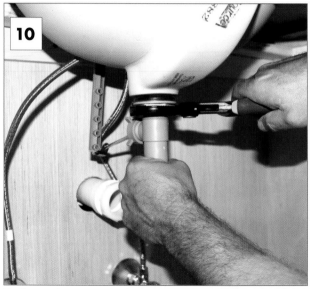

9 Wrap Teflon over the pop-up drain tube assembly twice before installing it into the threaded drain flange. Take care not to cover the cross holes for the pop-up lever.

10 Use the groove lock pliers to tighten the hex nut of the pop-up drain tube. This will put pressure on the clear flat plastic washer and compress the rubber washer under the sink for a watertight seal. This will push out the excess plumber's putty or silicone caulk on the sink side, and you will need to clean it from around the chrome flange.

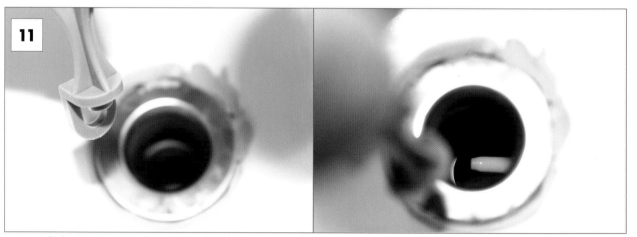

11 With the pop-up lever loosely installed in the pop-up drain tube, insert the pop-up drain stopper into the chrome sink flange on the sink side and align the slot of the stopper to the end of the cross-lever pin. Tighten the pop-up cross-lever compression nut and install the metal spring clip so the vertical adjustment bar from the drain lever is between the two ends of the spring clip.

> **✓ TIP**
>
> Some of the best plumbers I have worked with leave a bucket under the drain assembly in the cabinet overnight just in case a leak occurs later. This prevents the bottom of the wooden cabinet from becoming ruined. If the bucket is empty the next day, you know you're home free on this repair!

12 Reinstall the compression nut and the plastic compression washer from the J-bend of the P-trap onto the bottom end of the pop-up drain tube. Reassemble the clean P-trap J-bend and 7-inch wall tube with the compression nuts and install the end into the trap adapter of the drain line. Snug all of the compression nuts at each joint. Turn the hot and cold water valve stops on under the sink or at the main water valve. Place a paper towel under the sink drain. Run the cold water only and check for leaks. If any occur, retighten the compression nuts and wipe the joint dry before testing again. Next, run the hot water only to check for leaks in the same manner. Lastly, place the empty bucket back under the sink and pull the pop-up drain handle to close the drain stopper. Fill the sink with water halfway. Check the underside of the sink at the rubber washer seal. If water is present, retighten the hex nut with the groove lock pliers to compress the rubber seal more. Wipe any leaks dry with paper towels to distinguish from subsequent leaks.

VANITY DRAIN P-TRAP

SKILL LEVEL

- **Basic**

TOOLS REQUIRED

- **Small bucket**
- **Groove lock pliers**
- **Paper towels**

The vanity sink drain is often the culprit of standing water in the sink or slow-draining water. Neither of these two conditions is desirable, especially at times when everyone needs to use the sink, such as in the morning.

The drain will clog over time from hair, soap scum, and the occasional object that falls into the sink and—*swoosh*—down the drain it goes. The drain's inside diameter becomes smaller and smaller as more hair and soap scum build up slowly.

Advertisements will lead you to believe that your drain can be unclogged magically if you purchase a certain type of drain cleaner. Don't get me wrong—sometimes it works, but, many times, the first, second, or third bottle may *not* do the trick.

The P-trap for a bathroom sink can be either chrome-plated brass or PVC. The PVC type is preferred if the property is known to have hard water.

There are two styles of the common P-trap. The differences are the materials they are made from and the compression washers that each works best with. When the P-trap is exposed under wall-mounted sinks or behind pedestal sinks, the chrome finish model is preferred. When the P-trap is hidden inside a vanity that has doors, the PVC type is used. The PVC type is also preferred if the property is known to have hard water. Note: Be sure to take the defective part with you for comparison when shopping for a replacement. P-traps come in two different sizes; the 1¼-inch size is for vanity sinks.

The easiest way to clean the P-trap drain for a bathroom sink is to disassemble the trap completely. This way, you will be able to see where the clog is and how much the inside diameter of the trap has been reduced by buildup.

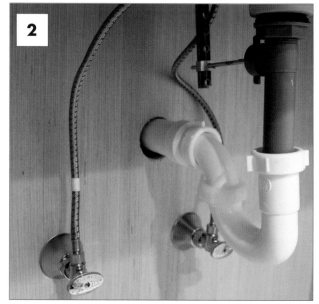

1 First, turn the valve stops off under the vanity for the hot and cold water. If the vanity sink does not have valve stops, locate the main water valve and turn that off. This is to prevent anyone from accidentally turning on the water while you are removing the P-trap. Place a small bucket under the J-bend of the P-trap. This will catch any water that is backed up inside the vertical pop-up drain tube, and it will also allow the water in the J-bend to drain into the bucket and not spill in the cabinet or on the floor. Loosen the top compression nut of the P-trap. Loosen the compression nut at the trap adapter; also loosen the compression nut between the 7-inch wall tube and the J-bend so you can remove the J-bend from the cabinet. Drain the trap water into the bucket. At this time, check the open end of the tailpiece of the pop-up for clogs.

2 Next, remove the 7-inch wall tube from the trap adapter so that you can check the pipe opening at the trap adapter for clogs. With all of the P-trap pieces removed, take them outside or to a utility sink and clean any buildup from inside of the trap parts. Also check the compression ring that seals the top of the J-bend to the tailpiece of the pop-up drain. If this is bad, replace it with a new one. Reinstall the cleaned P-trap 7-inch wall tube with the compression nut over the open end of the pipe that is inserted into the trap adapter. Insert the top of the J-bend over the tailpiece of the pop-up drain with the compression nut and ring already in place. Align the threads of all of the joints. To prevent cross-threading the compression nuts, rotate the nut counterclockwise until you hear a click. Rotate the compression nut clockwise and hand-tighten. Place a paper towel under the reinstalled P-trap. Turn on the hot and cold valve stops or the main water valve. Run only the cold water to check for leaks. If leaks occur, retighten the compression rings but *do not* overtighten them. Wipe the joint dry with a paper towel to distinguish between subsequent leaks. Finally, run only the hot water to check for leaks using the same process.

For chrome metal P-traps, the instructions are the same. The washer between the J-bend and 7-inch wall tube is a flat rubber washer. The washer at the top of the J-bend over the tailpiece of the pop-up drain can be a flat rubber or plastic tapered washer (see Step 1 on page 119).

When installing the chrome metal P-trap, the compression nut threads can become cross-threaded. Be sure to align the threads and rotate the nut backward until you hear a click. Then rotate the nut clockwise and tighten by hand. Compression nuts for chrome metal P-traps require you to tighten them completely with groove lock pliers after hand-tightening. Caution: *Do not* over tighten. Only a half to a three-quarter turn with a tool is required beyond hand-tightening.

Vanity Drain P-Trap

BATHTUB WASTE AND OVERFLOW

SKILL LEVEL

- **Semiskilled**

TOOLS REQUIRED

- **Four-way screwdriver**
- **Adjustable wrench**

MATERIALS REQUIRED

- **New tip-toe drain-stopper assembly or new trip-lever assembly**

The bathtub drain's operation is straightforward process, yet one that can become problematic if soap residue, hair debris, and other issues cause clogs. Many homes have only one bathtub, which can mean 100 gallons of water going through the bathtub drain on any given day with a family of four. When the water doesn't drain correctly, it will quickly back up around the drain and continue to fill up the tub.

A bathtub drain is closed by one of two methods:

Toe-tip spring-loaded drain stopper

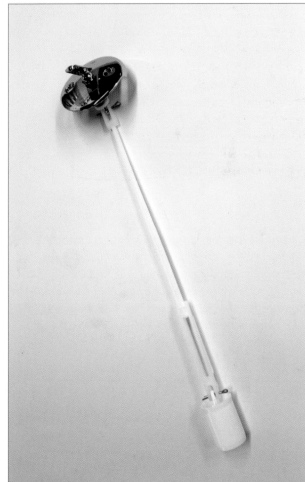

Trip-lever drain-stopper float

Chapter 14 | Bathroom Plumbing Repairs

Bathtub Waste and Overflow

REPLACING A TOE-TIP SPRING-LOADED DRAIN STOPPER

It is easier to determine if a toe-tip spring-loaded drain stopper is operating effectively because the water is stopped in the tub at the top of the drain. Push down the spring-loaded drain stopper to prevent water from entering the drain. If any water is getting past the drain stopper, you will be able to see it flowing underneath the drain stopper and/or hear it trickling down the drain.

If the spring-loaded drain stopper is no longer operating correctly, you can find a replacement at the local home-supply center. Grip the spring-loaded drain stopper and rotate it counterclockwise until it unthreads, and remove it from the drain strainer. Note: It is a good idea, if possible, to take the existing drain stopper with you to match the thread size with the existing drain strainer. If the thread size is different, you will need to replace the chrome drain strainer; luckily, kits also include this part.

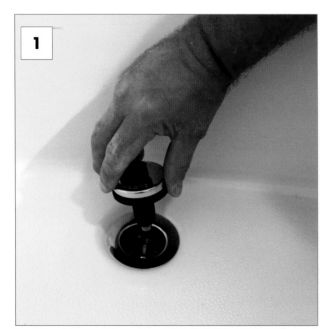

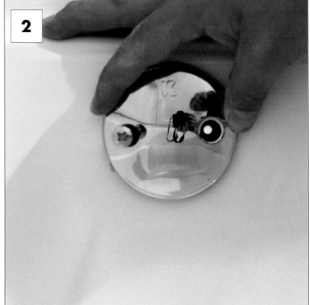

1 Insert the new toe-tip spring-loaded drain stopper by threading the stopper in a clockwise motion. Press the top of the stopper to close the drain. Fill the tub with enough warm water to cover the bottom of the tub surface. Stop the flow of water and check the drain stopper by looking for water flowing to the drain and/or listening for the sound of water trickling down the drain. If this occurs, the drain stopper is defective, and you should exchange it for a new one at the home-supply center.

2 When replacing the toe-tip drain stopper, the kit may also come with a new blank overflow plate with chrome truss-head screws. Remove the existing screws and the old blank overflow plate. Replace with the new blank overflow plate and tighten the new screws. This gives the new-look appearance inside the tub.

THE TRIP-LEVER DRAIN SYSTEM

When the tub won't drain properly or completely, and it has the trip-lever drain system, the first thing to check is the condition of the tub drain strainer cover. This cover is the first item in the drain assembly to stop the drain from being clogged with hair clumps and other buildup.

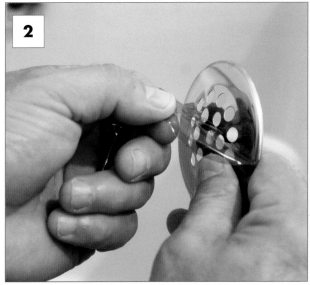

2 Look inside the tub strainer for further drain obstructions. If present, remove them with a rag or paper towel. Installing a new tub strainer cover will improve the appearance and drain function. Remove the plastic film that protects the finish from scratching. Place the cover over the drain strainer, insert the new chrome truss-head screw into the tub strainer, and tighten by hand with a four-way screwdriver. Close the trip waste lever by pulling up on the lever. Run warm water to cover the bottom of the tub. Open the trip waste lever by pushing down on the lever. Observe the flow of water toward the drain with the new strainer cover installed.

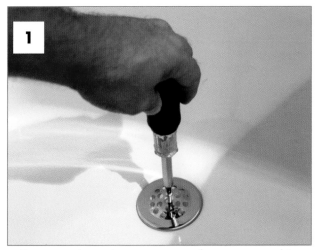

1 To remove the strainer cover, use a four-way screwdriver to loosen and remove the screw in the center of the cover.

Additional Drain System Problems

There can be many different issues with a trip-lever tub drain stopper. First, the drain can get clogged with soap residue and hair, preventing the trip-lever drain-stopper float to assume its correct closed position.

Another issue with this style of drain stopper is that, if the drain-stopper float is attached to a brass chain, the chain may be twisted or obstructed, not permitting the drain-stopper float to be positioned correctly.

Lastly, the trip lever may not be working correctly. The cotter pin connecting the threaded rod or chain of the drain-stopper float can be missing, corroded, or otherwise preventing correct operation.

1 To investigate problems with the trip-lever drain-stopper assembly, loosen and remove the two chrome truss-head slotted screw holding the chrome overflow plate.

Chapter 14 | Bathroom Plumbing Repairs

2 With the two screws removed, gently pull the overflow plate up and away from the tub and start to pull out the rod connected to the drain-stopper float. Inspect the condition of the cotter pin on the back of the overflow plate and replace if necessary.

3 Continue to carefully pull the remaining length of the drain-stopper float rod and remove the assembly for further inspection and cleaning. If the flow of tub water is not being stopped at the drain, you may need to adjust the drain-stopper float rod.

4 Loosen the hex jam nuts that secure the threaded rod into the round housing for brass models. To extend the float for brass and plastic rods, turn the threaded rod counterclockwise when looking down on the rod from the cotter pin that connects the rod to the trip lever. Note: To raise the drain-stopper float, turn the rod clockwise when looking down on the rod from the cotter pin. Reinsert the trip-lever assembly with the drain-stopper float attached carefully into the overflow tube. Install the overflow plate screws and tighten lightly to check the operation of the trip-lever drain-stopper float assembly. Pull the trip lever upward, which lowers the drain-stopper float into the overflow tube to close the drain. Run warm water to cover the bottom of the tub floor and check the flow of water. If water flows toward the drain and/or you hear water trickling down the drain, the float is not in the correct position to fully stop the water from draining. Readjust using the previous instructions.

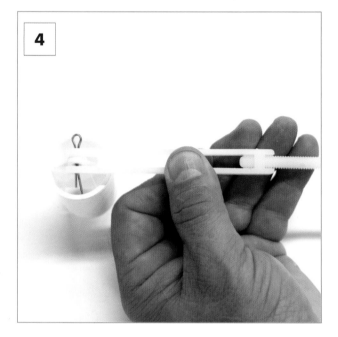

Chapter 14 | Bathroom Plumbing Repairs

Bathtub Waste and Overflow

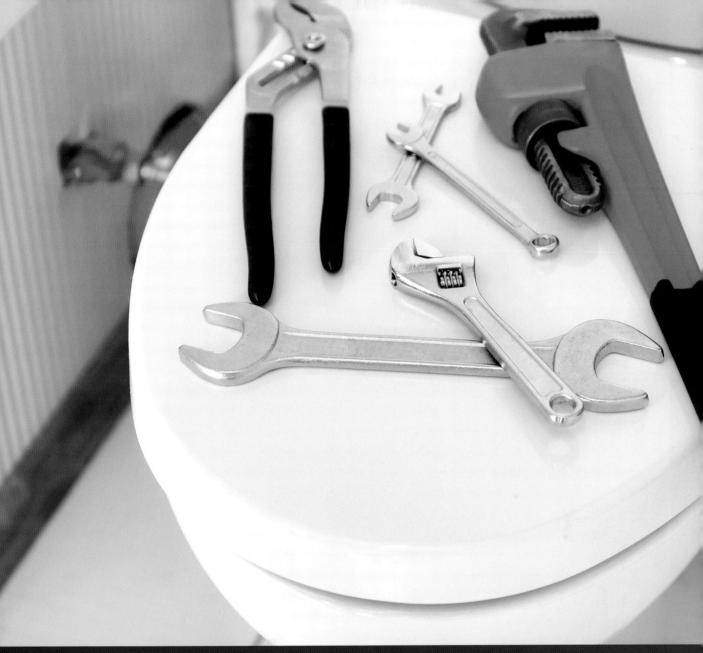

TOILET REPAIRS

WAX SEAL AND FLANGE BOLTS

SKILL LEVEL

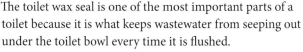

- **Skilled**

TOOLS REQUIRED

- **Small flat-head screwdriver**
- **Adjustable wrench or socket with ratchet**
- **Putty knife**
- **Plastic bag or scrap plywood**
- **Trash bag**
- **Disposable gloves**
- **Rags or paper towels**
- **Trash can**
- **Hacksaw**
- **Small bucket**

MATERIALS REQUIRED

- **New wax ring with integral horn**
- **Kit containing new flange bolts**

The toilet wax seal is one of the most important parts of a toilet because it is what keeps wastewater from seeping out under the toilet bowl every time it is flushed.

Toilets obviously get a lot of use, especially in homes that have only one bathroom. I remember those days well! It seemed like someone was always in the bathroom when I needed to use it. In the house I grew up in, there was a toilet in the basement laundry, but who had time to go to the basement from the second floor? It seemed more logical to just bang on the door harder!

✓ TIP

The task of replacing the toilet wax seal and/or the two toilet bolts can be difficult for one person. It's much easier when another person is available to help.

1 Turn off the valve stop connected to the toilet. If this does not stop the water flow into the tank, turn off the main house valve. Remove the porcelain tank lid and place it out of the way. Flush the toilet and hold the flush handle down to remove as much water as possible from the tank. It is not necessary to remove all of the water. Using a wet/dry vacuum, remove any water from the bottom of the tank and the bottom of the bowl, including the trap.

Wax Seal and Flange Bolts

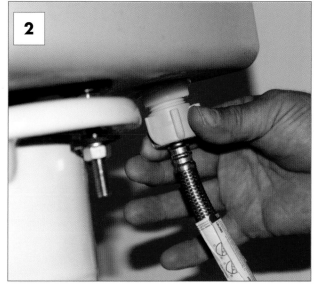

2 Disconnect the riser tube from the flush valve threads of the toilet.

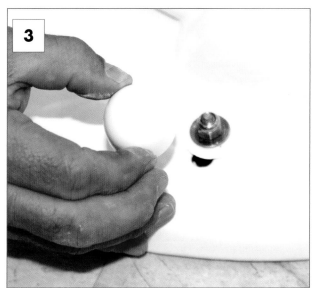

3 Use a small flat-head screwdriver to pry the mounting bolt caps off. Use an adjustable wrench or socket with a ratchet to loosen the mounting screw nuts and remove the plastic washer and brass washer. Straddle the toilet seat and lift the toilet with the tank attached straight up over the toilet flange. Place the toilet aside on a plastic bag or scrap plywood to protect the bathroom floor. Put on the disposable gloves and remove the existing wax seal from the toilet flange and the two mounting bolts. Clean any remaining wax off the toilet flange with rags or paper towels and discard these in the trash. Have your helper carefully tilt the toilet back so you can clean the bottom of the bowl flange with additional rags or paper towels; discard these in the trash.

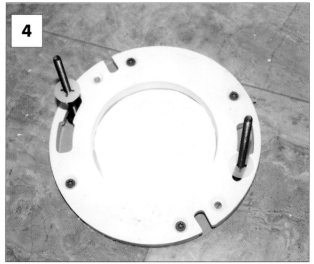

4 Install the new toilet flange bolts that are included with the wax seal. Use the plastic washers included to secure the bolts to the flange tightly and vertically.

5 Install the new wax seal over the toilet flange. Note: I recommend purchasing the type of wax seal with the horn attached to the wax ring to prevent leaks.

6 Straddle the toilet bowel and lift the toilet over the wax seal and bolts. Note: With your helper, guide the mounting bolts through the slotted holes in the bowl flange, lower the toilet, and compress the wax seal between the toilet flange and the bottom of the toilet. Attach the plastic cap washers "this side up" on top of the porcelain toilet bowl mounting flange. This plastic washer prevents the brass washer that is attached next from coming in contact with the porcelain and damaging it. Complete this step for both bolt locations.

7 Next, install the brass washer over the plastic washer. The brass washer will add more, with the plastic washer from the previous step, to secure the toilet in place on the toilet flange attached to the floor. Complete this step for both bolt locations.

8 Use a tape measure to set an equal distance between the back corners of the tank and the finished wall surface. Attach the hex nuts over the bolt and tighten securely at both bolt locations using an adjustable wrench or socket with a ratchet. Be careful not to overtighten and crack the porcelain toilet flange. Use a small bucket to pour water into the toilet, filling the trap and bottom of the bowl. Check for leaks. Tighten the hex nuts more if any leaks occur. Use a paper towel to dry any leaks at the floor and the toilet flange to distinguish from subsequent leaks. Refill the small bucket with water and dump it into the toilet bowl. This action will overflow the trap and effectively flush the toilet. Again, check for any leaks.

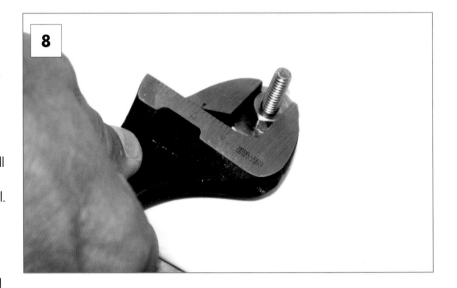

Wax Seal and Flange Bolts

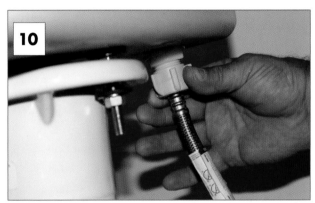

9 Cut the new brass toilet bowl mounting bolts above the hex nuts with a hacksaw so that you can snap the plastic trim caps onto the plastic washers. Place the plastic caps back over the hex nuts and push down until you hear a click, which means that they are securely attached to the plastic washers.

10 Reconnect the riser tube to the flush valve threads of the toilet. Turn the valve stops or the main house valve back on. Fill the tank with water. When the water inlet valve stops filling the tank, push the flush handle down to flush a full tank of water through the bowl. Check again for any leaks. Replace the porcelain tank lid on the tank. Congratulations! Your repair is complete.

FLANGE

SKILL LEVEL

- Semiskilled

TOOLS REQUIRED

- **Adjustable wrench or socket with a ratchet**
- **Small flat-head screwdriver**
- **Putty knife**
- **Hacksaw**
- **Disposable gloves**
- **Rags or paper towels**
- **Trash can**
- **Small bucket**

MATERIALS REQUIRED

- **Flange repair kit**
- **New wax ring with integral horn**
- **Kit containing new toilet bolts**

Toilet flange failures can occur for various reasons. The older the home is, the more likely the flange will be made of cast iron. The cast iron flange is connected to the 3- or 4-inch drain pipe by a method using oakum and melted lead.

A licensed plumber can repair and or replace cast-iron toilet flanges. However, the industry has developed several different types of parts available for a less expensive and less time-consuming repair.

As I mentioned in the Wax Seal and Flange Bolt section, a toilet in a home is used extensively, especially when the home has only one toilet.

It's always best to have a helper who has some experience working with toilets when removing one for the first time. I wish someone would have told that to my two sons-in-law when they decided to remove the toilet in a very small powder room. Their idea was to discard the toilet and get a new one, but I guess they didn't think far enough ahead to know that the flange connected to the cast-iron pipe needed to stay with the house. Yep, you guessed it—they cracked the cast-iron flange!

Of course, their only plan was to get me to repair it. Boy, did I let those two have it, telling them that the flange was ruined and that it was going to be a very expensive repair. Little did they know that I could get the parts for less than $15 if the pipe itself was still good. It was, and I completed the repair in about an hour, including going to the home-supply center!

Follow the instructions in the Wax Seal and Flange Bolt section. This includes the "fun" parts of removing the old wax seal and existing flange bolts.

Take a picture of the damaged flange to bring to the home-supply center with you along with a list of needed parts. Many times, the person working in the plumbing department will be familiar with this repair. After purchasing the flange repair parts, unpack them and assess the orientation of the existing slotted flange bolt openings. The flange repair kit has two metal halves of equal size that can be used separately or together. There is also a complete ring available that will not separate.

With the two-piece flange repair kit, you will use both halves for the repair. Be careful when sliding them together. One half has raised tabs at the slots, and the other half has straight tabs to slide under the raised ones. You will also need to install new flange bolts in the repair flange, and some kits come with these bolts. Others do not include them, but they are available in wax ring kits at the home-supply center.

Use the six recessed holes on the top of the flange to screw the new flange to the wood deck with ceramic-coated wood screws. It may be necessary to drill holes through the original flange to allow the six screws to go through it.

Flange repair parts.

Be careful when sliding the two-piece flange together.

FLUSH HANDLE

SKILL LEVEL

• Basic

TOOLS REQUIRED

• Groove lock pliers (only if the hex nut on the inside of tank cannot be loosened by hand)

MATERIALS REQUIRED

• New flush handle assembly

Toilet tank flush handles have a tendency to break after an extended period of time. If you think about how often the toilet is flushed after someone uses it or even just during routine cleaning, that is a lot of stress on the flush handle.

Many older toilets used metal for the entire handle and lever arm. These were actually some of the best made parts, and replacement parts with a chrome plastic flush handle and metal lever arm are available. To keep costs down, you can buy a replacement with the entire handle assembly made of plastic, which I *do not* prefer.

Carefully lift the porcelain tank lid and set it somewhere out of the way. Determine the flush handle problem. If the chain or the attachment nut came off, you probably only need to reattach it, and your repair will be complete. If the arm attached to the flush handle is plastic and broken,

you'll need a new flush handle assembly. I suggest replacing it with a model that has a metal arm.

If the chain has broken, most likely it has corroded, and you will need a new one. The chain is usually not sold separately but is sold with the flapper valve for the flush valve assembly. (See the Flapper Valve section.)

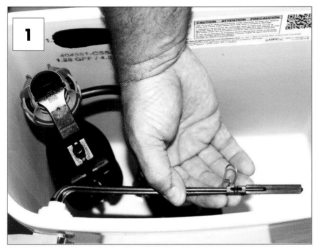

1 Remove the chain from the flush handle assembly. Unscrew the attachment nut inside the front tank wall that secures the flush handle assembly.

2 Slide the old flush handle assembly through the square opening in the front tank wall and take it with you to the home-supply center to replace.

Flush Handle

3 Remove the nut from the new flush handle assembly and install the new handle through the square opening in the front tank wall

4 Make sure that the square part of the handle is engaged in the square opening. Attach the nut to secure the handle and tighten *by hand only!* Make sure that the flush handle lever arm is horizontal when tightening the nut. Attach the existing chain to the flush handle arm so the chain has little slack in it when no pressure is applied to the flush handle. Push down on the new flush handle to check the flushing operation. If the toilet flushes correctly, reinstall the porcelain tank lid. Say good-bye to problems with the old tank flush handle. Bet you're **not** going to miss them!

FLAPPER VALVE

SKILL LEVEL

- **Basic**
  (be careful when working around porcelain fixtures)

TOOLS REQUIRED

- **Rag or paper towel**
- **Trash can**
- **Small bucket**

MATERIALS REQUIRED

- **New flapper valve**

There are several issues you may experience with the flapper valve in the bottom of the toilet tank over time. To check for some of the most common issues, remove the porcelain tank lid and set it somewhere out of the way.

- **The chain becomes detached from the flush handle arm.** This is the easiest problem to deal with. If this is the case, just reconnect the chain and flush the toilet to ensure that the flapper valve moves with the flush handle.
- **The flush handle arm is broken.** Even though the flush handle moves on the outside of the tank, a broken flush handle arm will not pull the flapper valve open. (See the Flush Handle Replacement section.)
- **The chain is broken between the flapper valve and the flush handle arm.** Unfortunately, in this case, you'll need to purchase a new flapper valve.
- **The flapper valve no longer seals against the flapper valve body seat.** This occurs over time due to hard water minerals in the tank, age, and shrinkage of the rubber valves, which allows water from the tank to bypass it and flow into the toilet bowel.

This last issue is what creates the sound of water running intermittently. My youngest daughter can attest to being startled when that happens. I once found a bowl of cereal in the TV room but no one at home because she ran to the neighbor's house to tell them that she was certain someone was in the house!

This problem also causes your monthly water and sewer bills to increase—as well as the electric bill every time the well pump turns on unnecessarily!

1 Turn off the valve stop connected to the toilet. If this does not stop the water flow into the tank, locate and turn off the main house valve. Flush the toilet and hold the flush handle down to remove as much water as possible from the tank. It is *not* necessary to remove all the water.

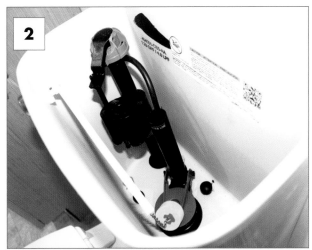

2 Unhook the chain end connected to the flush handle arm. Unhook the flapper valve from the two side pins attached to the vertical fill tube. Remove the existing flapper valve from the tank. Clean the opening of the valve seat of the vertical fill tub with a clean rag. Attach the new flapper valve to the two side pins of the vertical fill tube. Attach the chain to the flush handle arm. Check to be sure that the flapper valve covers the valve body opening completely before adding water back into the tank. Turn the valve stop or the main house valve back on. Allow the tank to fill normally with water to the required level. When the water inlet valve stops filling the tank, check the bowl to see if any water is seeping into the bowl. If so, the flapper is not sealing against the flush valve body seat opening in the bottom of the tank. (See the Flush Valve Replacement section.)

If the flapper valve seals without leaking, replace the porcelain tank lid on the tank. Hold the flush lever down to complete one flush cycle of the toilet. Congratulations! You have fixed one of the toilet's slowest, but most expensive, leaks!

Chapter 15 | Toilet Repairs

FLUSH VALVE

SKILL LEVEL

- Semiskilled

TOOLS REQUIRED

- Long flat-head screwdriver
- Adjustable wrench or socket with a ratchet
- Groove lock pliers
- Wet-dry vacuum
- Small bucket

MATERIALS REQUIRED

- New flush valve with new toilet tank bolt kit (bolts may be sold separately)

There are two styles of flush valve in use today. The original style is a ball float attached to a rod, and the ball rises and falls with the water level when the toilet is flushed. This allows the valve to open and the water to flow and fill the tank to the required water level. You adjust the flush valve by turning the fill-adjustment screw or by bending the rod. This type of flush valve is found mostly in 3-gallon flush tank models.

The second type of flush valve in use today is the vertical float style. When the toilet is flushed, the vertical float slides down the fill post. This allows the valve to open and the water to flow and fill the tank to the required water level. Adjustments at the flush valve are made by turning the fill-adjustment screw or by raising and lowering the telescopic height of the fill post. This style is found on all new 1.6-gallon tank models.

The flush valve located inside of the tank allows water to fill the tank after flushing and automatically stops the flow of water when the tank is at the required fill level.

The flush valve is submerged in the tank water except for the top part. The valve is subjected to the hard water minerals that take their toll on its parts. Most, if not all, of the valve is made of plastic.

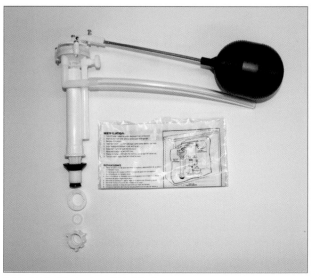

Original style of flush valve, with ball float.

Flush valve with vertical float.

1 Turn off the valve stop connected to the toilet. If this does not stop the water flow into the tank, locate and turn off main house valve. Flush the toilet and hold the flush handle down to remove as much water as possible from the tank. Using a wet-dry vacuum, remove the remaining amount of water in the tank.

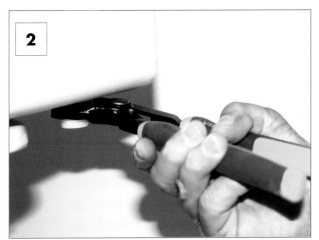

2 Loosen with an adjustable wrench and remove the top connection of the riser tube from the flush valve threads protruding through the bottom of the tank. Using an adjustable wrench, remove the hex nut at the bottom of the tank that secures the flush valve fill tube. Remove the existing flush valve body from the toilet, including the plastic fill tube line attached to the overflow tube.

3 Remove the new hex nut from the new flush valve assembly that you purchased. Install the new flush valve assembly. Be sure to connect the plastic fill tube to the overflow tube. Install the hex nut outside the bottom of the tank and tighten with an adjustable wrench. Tighten securely to seal the rubber washer inside the tank. Reinstall the top part of the riser tube that connects to the bottom threads of the flush valve protruding through the tank. Tighten securely. Use a small bucket to fill the bottom of the tank with 2 to 3 inches of water. Check for leaks where the flush valve gasket inside the tank is sealed by the plastic hex nut outside of the tank. Tighten the hex nut if leaks occur. Wipe any leaks dry with a paper towel to distinguish between subsequent leaks. Turn the valve stop or the main house back on. Allow the tank to fill naturally until the water-inlet valve stops the flow. Hold the flush handle down and allow the toilet to complete one normal flush cycle. Check again for any leaks between the tank bottom and the plastic hex nut and at the connection of the riser tube to the flush valve threads. If any leaks are detected, tighten the connections more. Wipe any leaks dry with a paper towel to distinguish between subsequent leaks. Place the porcelain tank lid back on top of the tank.

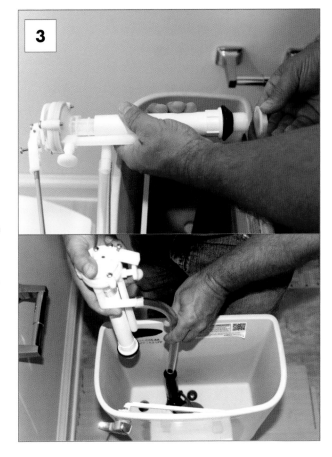

Chapter 15 | Toilet Repairs

FLUSH VALVE BODY GASKET AND TANK BOLT REPLACEMENT

SKILL LEVEL

- Semiskilled

TOOLS REQUIRED

- Long flat-head screwdriver
- Adjustable wrench or socket with a ratchet
- Groove lock pliers
- Wet-dry vacuum
- Small bucket

MATERIALS REQUIRED

- New flush valve body gasket
- New kit with tank bolts

The flush valve body gasket located on the outside bottom of the tank serves two purposes: on two-piece toilets, it seals the water tank and the toilet bowl deck where it is mounted, and it also provides a rubber cushion between two pieces of porcelain.

Over time, the rubber gasket becomes brittle, and leaks can occur between the water tank and the toilet bowl mounting deck. If you have ever placed the china plates back into the cabinet a little too roughly or slid two plates together, you get the sound and feel of fingernails on a slate chalkboard! Porcelain is hard yet as fragile as fine china plates. We know how delicately we have to treat both!

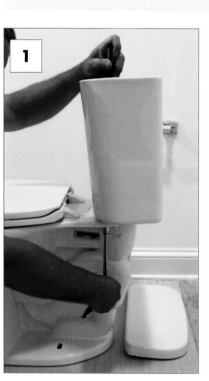

1 Turn off the valve stop connected to the toilet. If this does not stop the water flow into the tank, turn off the main house valve. Flush the toilet and hold the flush handle down to remove as much water as possible from the tank. Remove the porcelain tank lid and place it out of the way. Using a wet-dry vacuum, remove the remaining amount of water in the tank. Locate the brass hex nuts under the mounting deck of the toilet bowl and then loosen and remove them. If the tank bolts rotate when loosening the hex nuts, use a long screwdriver to prevent rotation. Exercise care when removing the porcelain tank to *not* damage the bowl or tank.

3 Take the worn parts with you to the home-supply center for replacements. Reinstall the new flush valve gasket onto the flush valve body protruding through the bottom of the tank while the tank is upside-down on the floor. Install the new tank bolts with the rubber washers under the bolt heads and the washers and hex nuts under the tank bottom. Tighten securely and carefully. Place the tank upright over the mounting deck of the bowl and align the tank-mounting screws over the holes on the mounting deck. Install the brass flat washers and hex nuts. Tighten by hand and make sure that the tank is level. Be sure to mount the tank parallel to the wall surface. Take measurements at each end. They must be equal to allow the porcelain tank lid to fit properly. Use a socket wrench or nut driver to tighten the nuts securely to compress the flush valve body seal.

2 Turn the tank over and place it on a towel or other soft material on the bathroom floor. Remove the flush valve body seal. This is located in the center of the bottom of the tank. Inspect the flush valve body for wear or corrosion. In addition, check the condition of the tank's brass bolt heads and rubber washers for wear or corrosion. It is worth the time to remove these parts using a flat-head screwdriver and adjustable wrench.

Use a small bucket to fill the tank with 2 to 3 inches of water. Check for any leaks between the tank bottom and the mounting deck of the bowl. Turn the valve stop or the main house valve back on. Allow the tank to fill naturally until the water-inlet valve stops the flow. Hold the flush handle down and allow the toilet to complete one normal flush cycle.

Check again for leaks between the tank bottom and the bowl. If you detect any leaks, tighten the brass hex nuts under the mounting deck of the bowl more. Be careful not to overtighten and crack the porcelain mounting deck. Wipe any leaks dry with a paper towel to distinguish between subsequent leaks. Replace the porcelain tank lid on top of the tank.

Chapter 15 | Toilet Repairs

Flush Valve Body Gasket and Tank Bolt Replacement

TOILET SEAT

SKILL LEVEL

- **Basic**

TOOLS REQUIRED

- **Four-way screwdriver**
- **Adjustable wrench**

MATERIALS REQUIRED

- **New toilet seat**
- **Paper towels**

Toilet seats are easy to replace or, if needed, just to retighten so they are safe to use. Many seats will become cracked over time from the chemicals used to clean them—not to mention the number of times people sit on them! Whatever the reason, be it style, function, or fit, there is more to buying a replacement toilet seat than you might think.

The number-one item to consider before purchasing a new seat is which style you need. Toilets have two different profiles: the traditional round front and the newer oblong front. It's easy to tell the difference because the oblong style extends farther away from the back wall, where the tank is located, and it also has a smaller radius along the front than a round model.

Another consideration is if you want to replace the current solid wood or plastic seat with a padded seat. Lastly, consider the color of the seat. The best way to match the color of the seat to that of the toilet is to stay with the manufacturer of the toilet. The manufacturer's name is usually stamped on the top of the bowl, where the toilet seat bolts are located, inside the flush tank, or even under the tank lid. One company's bone color may be entirely different than another company's bone color!

To replace or tighten the toilet seat, pull open the covers that conceal the screw heads.

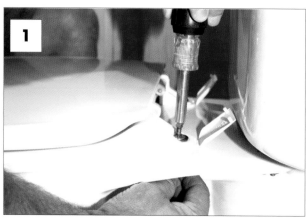

1 Use a screwdriver to loosen the seat-mounting bolts and reach under the seat-mounting deck of the bowl to prevent the plastic hex nuts from turning, either by hand or with an adjustable wrench. Remove the entire seat from the toilet and set aside. Cleaning the seat-mounting deck of the toilet bowl is a good idea, as dirt and dust get trapped around the seat screw mounting blocks.

2 Remove the new seat from its packaging and set on top of the toilet bowl. *Be sure the seat profile matches the toilet bowl profile.* Locate the metal reinforcing washers and install them over each hole where the mounting screws will be installed.

3 Install the new seat screws through the top of the seat mounting blocks. Then, install the plastic hex nuts under the seat-mounting deck of the toilet bowl flange and tighten by hand. Align the toilet seat edges with the toilet bowl. Finish tightening the toilet seat bolts until the seat is secure. Close the caps to conceal the toilet seat screws. Your seat is ready for use.

3

> ✓ **TIP**
>
> If you are just tightening a loose seat, turn the screwdriver clockwise until the bolts are tight again. You may also require an adjustable wrench to hold the plastic hex nuts. Then, close the caps to conceal the screw heads.

WATER LINE CONNECTIONS

SKILL LEVEL

- **Basic**

TOOLS REQUIRED

- **Groove lock pliers**
- **Adjustable wrench**
- **Wet-dry vacuum**

MATERIALS REQUIRED

- **New ⅜-inch riser tube**
- **New valve stop (if original needs to be replaced)**

The toilet riser tube will probably be the original one installed unless the original riser tube corroded and was replaced over the years. In the instructions for the various toilet repairs, we have covered how to remove the toilet riser tube and reconnect it. At some point, you will likely have to replace this part.

Today, there are two very good choices for the replacement part of this tube: one is the CPVC version to directly replace the chrome-plated original one, and the other is the stainless-steel flex hose.

Chapter 15 | Toilet Repairs

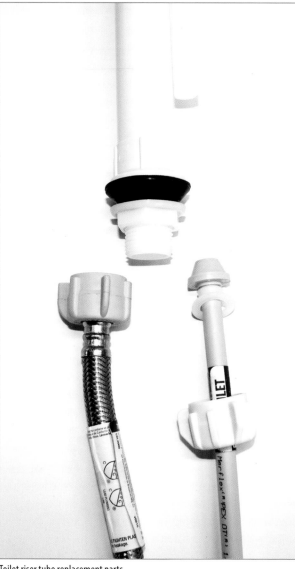

Toilet riser tube replacement parts.

Begin by turning off the water at the valve stop. If that doesn't stop the flow of water, locate and turn off the main water valve for the house. Note: If the existing valve stop begins to leak when you close it (for the first time since who knows when), you will need to replace it. If the valve stop has a threaded connection, it can be replaced easily. Follow the instructions in the Water Line Connections section. *However, if it is a soldered connection, contact your property owner to hire a qualified plumber to handle the repair.*

Remove the porcelain tank lid and carefully set aside. Hold the flush handle down until the water in the tank drains into the toilet bowl. Use a wet-dry vacuum to remove the remaining tank water. Using an adjustable wrench or groove lock pliers, loosen the nut that secures the toilet water line to the flush valve threads protruding out of the tank bottom. Using an adjustable wrench, loosen and remove the hex nut that connects the toilet water line to the valve stop.

Install the new stainless flex hose by attaching the end to the flush valve threads first and then tightening by hand. Create a loop to shorten the hose to connect the ⅜-inch compression end to the existing valve stop. Tighten both hex nuts completely to create a watertight seal. Note: The new stainless-steel flex hose has compression nuts at both end. Discard the original ⅜-inch nut and compression ring with the old water line.

CHAPTER 16
APPLIANCES

RANGE HOOD

SKILL LEVEL

- Basic

TOOLS REQUIRED

- Four-way screwdriver

MATERIALS REQUIRED

- New light bulb (maximum 60 watts)

Electric range hoods are available in two types: one with a metal duct to exhaust the heat and moisture to the outside, and one that is ductless and uses filters to recycle the heat and moisture back into the room.

The fan and light operations are controlled by switches on the front panel. The fan switch usually has two speeds. Both types of range hood attach to the bottom of the range cabinet with four screws. The electric supplied to both types is hard wired with the wire connections located in the junction box attached to the underside of the range hood with a screw. The wires are connected using wire nut caps that attach the line wires and neutral wires. The bare copper ground wire is attached to the green ground terminal screw.

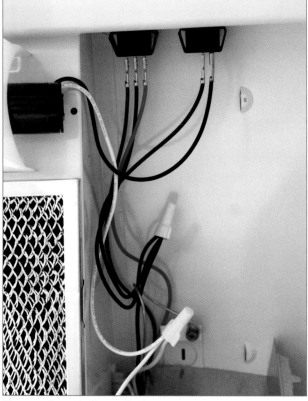

Wire connections under the range hood.

Range hood, attached by screws.

Because the ductless model is easier to install, many kitchens have this type. The filter in this type is very easy to remove, clean, and reinstall and is located under the range hood. The plastic clip at the top of the filter pivots so the filter will drop down. After cleaning, reinstall the filter by placing the bottom in first, then pushing the top upward, and then rotating the plastic clip to lock in place.

Both range hood models have a standard light bulb behind a plastic shield that protects the bulb from the effects of cooking on the stove. The plastic shield is easily removed by squeezing the sides to disengage the plastic tabs from the slots under the range hood. Unscrew the bulb and replace it with a new one of 60 watts or less so as not to overheat the plastic shield. Reinstall the shield by squeezing the sides and releasing the pressure so the tabs reengage in the slots.

Filters are easy to remove, clean, and reinstall.

Replace the bulb when it fails.

DISHWASHER

A plumber can make a dishwasher water line several ways during the original installation of the dishwasher. Some use a ⅜-inch flexible copper line soldered from a tee behind the wall or attached to a tee under the kitchen sink cabinet from the hot-water line of the faucet.

As seen here (top right), a two-way compression valve stop is connected to the hot-water line of the sink faucet. The left stainless flex hose is connected to the hot-water side of the faucet. The right stainless flex hose is connected to the dishwasher. Both the faucet and the dishwasher can be serviced independently of each other if needed, without having to turn off the house's main water valve.

The dishwasher drain line is connected to the sink drain tailpiece that has a hose tee configuration. The drain hose is held in place with a stainless-steel worm clamp. If the drain hose were to leak, you would retighten the worm clamp with a flat-head screwdriver.

If a leak were to continue where the drain hose connects to the tailpiece of the sink drain, you would unscrew the worm clamp and remove the drain hose, using a small bucket to drain the excess water in the drain hose. Inspect the tailpiece at the tee for the hose connection. Many times, this becomes corroded and needs to be replaced. See the Kitchen Sink Drain P-Trap section.

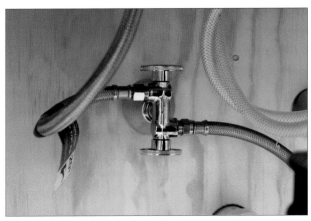

Two-way compression valve connected to hot-water line.

Tighten the worm clamp if the drain hose leaks.

Chapter 16 | Appliances

ELECTRIC HOT-WATER HEATER

SKILL LEVEL

- Skilled

TOOLS REQUIRED

- Electrical meter
- #2 Phillips screwdriver

MATERIAL REQUIRED

- None (You can troubleshoot, as explained here, but a licensed plumber will need to make any repairs or replacements.)

We have all been there: we're taking a hot shower, and partway through, the water turns cooler, and then cold, and then finally ice cold! Hot water differences in older homes is not uncommon, especially when someone turns on the water elsewhere in the house. However, a pattern of temperature changes when doing dishes or taking a shower can be from a water heater not operating correctly.

For an electric water heater to operate efficiently, it requires two heating elements, each with its own thermostat, to heat the water. When a heating element goes bad, mineral scale from the water begins to build up on the element. The more buildup, the less efficiently the element operates, until it eventually breaks. When this happens, the only indication is that the hot water doesn't last as long or the recovery period to heat more water takes longer.

1 To check if an element in the upper or lower position is going bad or has stopped working altogether, you must locate the breaker or fuse that operates the water heater. Turn the breaker off or remove the fuse in the fuse box. Loosen and remove the screws at the element door for the upper and lower positions and remove the covers.

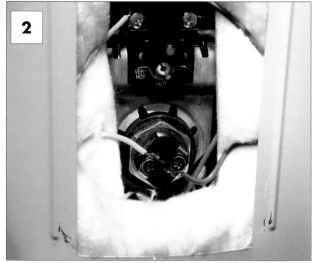

2 Expose the element terminal connections by pushing the tank insulation out of the way.

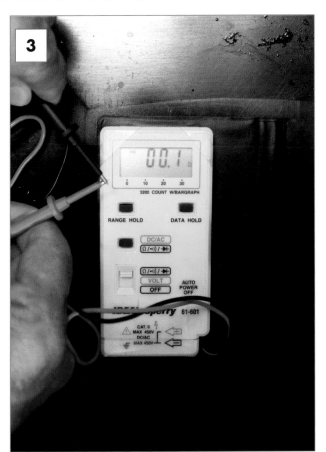

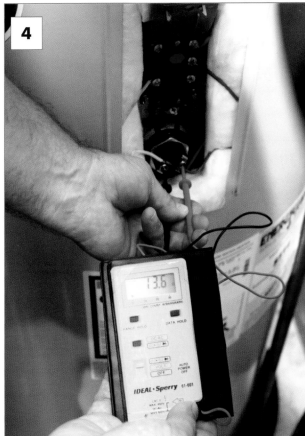

3 Turn the electrical meter on and set it to Ohms to check continuity. To check the meter for correct setting and operation, touch the test leads together. A very low output reading should display; most test meters also emit an audible beep when checking for continuity.

4 Touch one test lead to each of the two terminal screws and check to see if the element reads for continuity (and listen for the beep, if applicable). If the element reads "open" using the meter, then the element could be the reason for no hot water.

> **✓ TIP**
>
> If an element needs to be replaced, contact the property owner or his designated plumber (with the property owner's permission) to handle the repair correctly, efficiently, and safely. Replace the element covers and turn on the breaker or place the fuse back into the fuse box to power the water heater.

Chapter 16 | Appliances

HOT-AIR FURNACE

SKILL LEVEL

- **Basic**

TOOLS REQUIRED

- **None**

MATERIALS REQUIRED

- **New air filter of correct type and size**

Every hot-air furnace will have a filter to trap the dust and other airborne particles inside the house. This filter, when changed on a regular schedule, can help the furnace operate at peak efficiency. A filter left too long in service will rob the hot-air system of performance and allow enormous amounts of dust to collect at the cold-air return registers.

For best results, determine if the property owner has a maintenance agreement with a heating contractor. If not, discuss with them purchasing the correct size and style of filter needed before beginning this task. This will ensure the correct filter is acquired and the correct method to change it is used.

1 Locate the thermostat that controls the hot-air furnace and turn the circulating fan to the off position. If the filter inside the filter housing is made of a plastic mesh material, this is a washable filter. Clean the filter with a garden hose outside. Allow the filter to thoroughly air-dry and then reinstall. Write down the date on which you cleaned the filter on a sheet near the furnace to keep track of the cleaning schedule.

2 Locate the hot-air furnace filter in the bottom or lower side of the unit for up-draft styles and above the unit for down-draft styles. The filter size may have been written on the filter access door by the installers. The filter access door should be labeled with a directional arrow. Open the filter door and remove the existing filter. This filter will also have an arrow printed on its cardboard frame. The arrows should be pointing in the same direction.

✓TIP

Be sure to reinstall the washable filter the same way it was installed before removing.

Chapter 16 | Appliances

3 Unwrap the new filter, mark the date of installation on the filter, and slide the filter into the filter box with the arrow matching the arrow on the filter box door. Close the filter door and make sure it seals tight. Turn the circulating fan on at the thermostat. Check for any air leaks at the filter door. Major leaks usually make a whistling sound.

CONDENSATE PUMP

SKILL LEVEL

- **Semiskilled**

TOOLS REQUIRED

- **4-way screwdriver**
- **Electrical meter or polarity plug tester**

MATERIALS REQUIRED

- **None (You can troubleshoot, as explained here, but a qualified technician will need to do the repair.)**

Indoor air handlers equipped with air conditioning coils known as A-coils must have a way for the excess moisture from the condensation process to be drained. In a normal setting, where the condensate drain line can be attached to the main drain exit of the house plumbing, gravity can accomplish this.

When the condensate drain line is located below the main drain exit, a condensate pump is installed to pump condensate water back up to the main drain exit line, and then gravity will drain the line normally from there. A condensate trap is installed in the drain line that exits from the air-handler chassis box. This trap is used to prevent backflow of sewer gases into the condensate line. It also creates an air seal from outdoor air when the condensate line exits through an exterior wall.

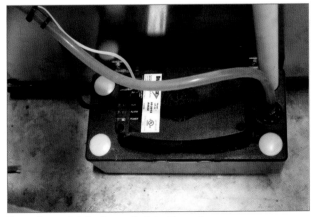

The condensate drain line is normally drained by gravity.

Chapter 16 | Appliances

The condensate trap can become clogged with scale from the condensate water, and then the drain will not work properly. When this occurs, it will be evident because extremely cold water will collect on the floor at the bottom of the air-handler chassis box. The water is dripping from the A-coil and then overflowing the condensate pan.

If the condensate trap appears *not* to be clogged, yet very cold water is collecting on the floor at the bottom of the air-handler chassis box, then you should check the condensate pump. Check the current at the outlet to which the condensate pump is connected. It should read 120 volts nominal.

Next, check the operation of the condensate pump. On the inlet side, add water to the condensate pump reservoir. The float should activate the pump to run. If the reservoir fills and the pump does not activate, the float and/or pump may be the issue. Note: In case of either of the two aforementioned problems, notify the property owner so he or she can hire a qualified repair technician.

A condensate trap prevents backflow of gases into the line.

CENTRAL AIR CONDITIONING UNIT

SKILL LEVEL

- Basic

TOOLS REQUIRED

- None

MATERIALS REQUIRED

- **Weatherproof cover for winter months (for central air conditioning outdoor units only)**

Maintaining an outdoor compressor unit for your central air conditioning system is fairly easy. Repairing the actual operation of the unit is a job for a licensed professional, but you should do routine cleaning and maintenance on a regular seasonal schedule.

First, keep your outdoor unit free of weeds, brush, and other debris around the sides and top. People generally try to disguise these units by planting bushes or plants near them. The unit relies on the free movement of air across the condensing coils for peak efficiency. The older models have a wire screen that protects the cooling fins from damage. Newer models have solid metal sides with openings for air movement.

Second, the outdoor unit's fan blade can become lodged if small limbs from nearby trees fall on top of it. Smaller twigs will be cut by the fan blades as they spin and will make a loud clang as they are being cut. This can damage the fan blade(s) or send the cut twig through the aluminum cooling fins, causing major damage.

Every outdoor unit is required to have an electrical disconnect fuse to interrupt power to the unit. The fuse inside this box is intended for the professional service technician. You can use this fuse in the event that your unit has malfunctioned, and the service company requires you to take the unit out of service until the technician arrives to repair it.

An outdoor unit for central air conditioning *only*—not one used with a heat pump furnace—should be covered with a waterproof cover during the offseason. The cover will protect the unit from fall foliage and winter ice and snow, and reduce the damage caused by the sun. *Be sure to remove this cover before you place the unit back in service for the warm months.*

An outdoor compressor unit for central air conditioning.

An electrical disconnect fuse for interrupting power when repairing the outdoor unit.

DRYER VENTS

SKILL LEVEL

- **Basic**

MATERIALS REQUIRED

- **Damp cloth or paper towels**

TOOLS REQUIRED

- **Wet-dry vacuum**
- **Extension cord**
- **Ladder (if the exhaust vent is above head height)**

A dryer vent provides a necessary means to expel the moisture from the clothes dryer to the outside atmosphere. Depending on the age and efficiency of the dryer, the moisture content and the temperature of the air that goes through the dryer vent line to the outside will vary.

If the dryer vent is in need of repair or replacement, you must use a metal type of flexible hose from the dryer exit point to the rigid duct. The older-style vinyl flexible hoses are no longer considered safe by many of the regulating bodies that deal with fire prevention. Note: To ensure that the dryer vent line remains free of clogged dryer lint, which can be flammable, locate the lint screen inside the dryer and clean the screen before every use. The location of the lint screen will vary depending in the manufacturer, model, and age of the dryer.

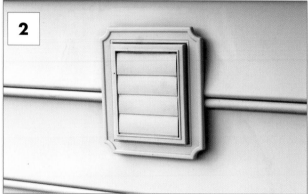

1 Turn the dryer on so that air flows through the dryer vent. Go outside and locate the dryer vent to be sure that the louvers or solid flap are open to let the air out.

2 Next, turn off the dryer and make sure that the louvers or solid flap close completely to seal off unwanted outside air and prevent animals from building nests inside the dryer vent.

DRYER VENTS WITH LOUVERS

A dryer vent with individual louvers that open when the dryer is running is the easiest type to clean. Do this when the outside temperature is above 75 degrees Fahrenheit, as this will make it easier to slightly bend the louvers to disengage the molded pins at each end.

1 As you remove each louver, be sure to clean all sides and edges with a damp cloth or paper towel.

2 Once you have removed all of the louvers, place a vacuum cleaner hose in the dryer vent pipe to clean out as much of the dryer lint that has accumulated at the end of the pipe as you can. Next, using a damp cloth or paper towel, finish cleaning the fine dryer lint dust that the vacuum didn't remove. Reinstall each plastic louver by engaging one side with the molded plastic pin, slightly bending the louver outward, and then engaging the molded plastic pin on the opposite side. Check the operation of each plastic louver by hand. To complete your dryer vent maintenance, turn the dryer back on and check the operation of the louvers to ensure that they operate correctly.

✓ TIP

To perform the same maintenance to a solid flap-style vent with a hood, follow each of the previous steps, but you will not be able to remove the solid flap because of the spring mounted to it.

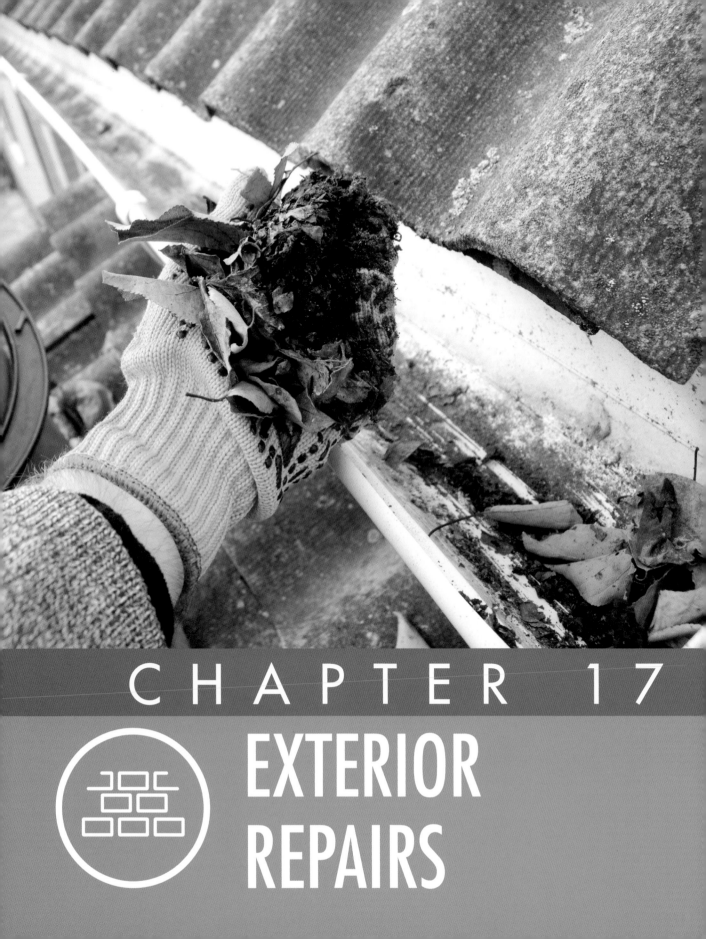

CHAPTER 17
EXTERIOR REPAIRS

BLACKTOP AND CONCRETE

SKILL LEVEL

- Basic

TOOLS REQUIRED

- Utility knife with sharp blades
- Caulk gun

MATERIALS REQUIRED

- Black Jack® roofing caulk
- Paint stir stick
- Long flat-headed nail
- Metal pin
- Electrical tape

Blacktop and concrete surfaces have several things in common, including the fact that they are both impervious surfaces, which means that water will not easily pass through them but instead will run off of them.

BLACKTOP

Blacktop is a popular choice for driveways and pathways. It consists of two layers:

- The base layer, which is made of coarse stone and bituminous oil. It is heated and then laid and flattened by a rolling machine.
- The finish layer, which is made of finer stone and bituminous oil, is heated and then applied over the base layer with the same rolling machine.

Because blacktop is only laid over a tamped 6-inch layer of crushed stone, the freezing temperatures in the winter will freeze the ground moisture as deep as 3 feet in the northeastern region. This freezing effect causes the ground to rise in the winter and then fall in the warmer spring weather, which creates a subtle movement of the blacktop that can, over time, lead to cracks in the surface.

1 Locate the crack(s) in the blacktop that need to be repaired.

2 Place the tube of Black Jack into the caulk gun and cut the tip with a utility knife to create a ¼-inch opening in the end of the tube. Insert a long, narrow pin into the open end of the tube and poke a hole in the foil seal at the top of the tube. Place the end of the caulk tube over the crack and begin to squeeze the trigger of the caulk gun to make the Black Jack flow into the crack. Note: To stop the flow of the caulk, press the release tab on the back of the caulk gun.

3 Continue filling the crack with caulk until the entire length is covered.

4 Use a thin, flat piece of wood, like a paint stir stick, to apply pressure to and flatten the caulk over the crack. Over time, the black oil-based caulk of the repaired crack will blend in to match the blacktop's color and texture. Note: Allow the caulk to dry for several hours in the sun on a warm day before driving over it with any vehicle.

5 If there is still some caulk left in the tube, place a nail with a flat head into the open end of the tube to help seal the end.

6 Wrap electrical tape over the nail head and around the caulk tube to create an airtight seal. This will prevent the contents from drying out for a period of time.

Chapter 17 | Exterior Repairs

Blacktop and Concrete

CONCRETE

SKILL LEVEL

- Basic

TOOLS REQUIRED

- Broom
- Utility knife with sharp blades
- Long pin
- Paint stir stick
- Small paintbrush
- Plastic spoon

MATERIALS REQUIRED

- Silicone caulk
- Colored sand to match the concrete color
  (You can purchase colored sand from a
  masonry-supply store.)

Concrete is another popular choice for porch floors, sidewalks, pathways, and driveways. It is composed of Portland cement, fine sand, and coarse stone. When mixed with water and reinforced with steel wire mesh or round rebar, this material is extremely strong. However, nothing has proven stronger than when the ground rises from the moisture freezing to depths of 3 feet in the northeast region. Combine that with when the ground falls with the warmer spring temperatures and it is a recipe for cracks and failures of concrete poured over 6 inches of tamped stone outside.

1 Locate the crack(s) to be repaired and use a broom to clean the area(s) thoroughly.

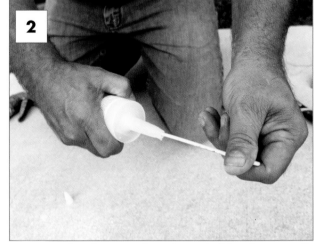

2 Remove the plastic cap from the end of the silicone-caulk tube. Cut the end of the caulk tube with a utility knife to create a ⅜-inch opening. Insert a long pin into the opening in the tube to poke a hole in the foil seal of the tube.

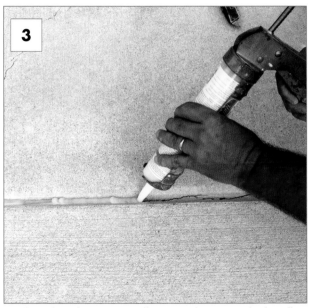

3 Place the tube into a caulk gun and squeeze the handle to apply a liberal amount of silicone along the length of the crack. Note: To stop the flow of the caulk, press the release tab on the back of the caulk gun.

4 Using your fingertip, push the silicone into the cracked area along the length of the crack. Place a liberal amount of colored sand over the silicone caulk in the crack.

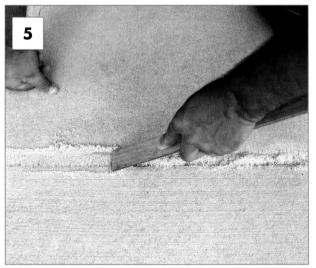

5 Apply pressure with a paint stir stick over the colored sand to help it adhere to the silicone caulk in the crack.

6 Use a plastic spoon to apply pressure over the colored sand to conform the sand and silicone caulk to the control joint of the concrete.

Blacktop and Concrete

Chapter 17 | Exterior Repairs

7 Scrape the excess from the edges and push it back into the control joint of the concrete to completely fill the joint.

8 Use a small paintbrush to remove any excess colored sand that did not adhere to the silicone caulk in the crack and control joint. The finished repair will require at least eight hours without rainfall to fully set up and cure. Place the cap back on the top of the silicone tube end to prevent the silicone from drying out.

POWER WASH EXTERIOR

SKILL LEVEL

- Semiskilled

TOOLS REQUIRED

- **Gas-powered or electric pressure washer (You can rent a pressure washer by the hour, day, or week from a home-supply center or tool-rental outlet. Also check with a neighbor, friend, or relative to see if borrowing one is possible.)**

MATERIALS REQUIRED

- **Gasoline for a gas-powered model or extension cords for an electric model (be sure that you plug your extension cord into a GFCI outlet)**
- **Cleaning solution (if needed)**

The home's exterior is affected by the seasonal climate changes and pollution in the atmosphere. Most people think that a hose, a brush, and cleaning solution will do just fine to clean the exterior. Unfortunately, that couldn't be further from the truth. The texture of exterior surfaces requires a specific size jet of water being sprayed under heavy water pressure measured in pounds per square inch (psi).

You must take extreme care that the water jet doesn't damage the surface of what you are cleaning. You also have to be careful to never spray any part of your body with the water jet from the nozzle. The water pressure isn't the issue as much as the impurities in the water and on your skin that will penetrate your skin and can cause severe infections in your body.

A gutter or downspout that leaks or overflows will generally leave an indicating sign for you to see. Many home foundation exteriors use brick, stone, and stucco as finished materials instead of just plain concrete blocks. You must be careful when cleaning any of these hard surfaces.

1 Using a high-pressure washer with the correct nozzle tip and at the proper distance from the wall can keep the house's exterior looking new. Always use the nozzle that will clean the surface with the least amount of pressure. Too much pressure can damage any surface, including concrete.

2 Always start at the upper area of a stain and work toward the bottom. Make sure to rinse the affected area without the trigger squeezed on the pressure gun handle so the area isn't reblasted with dirt from the bottom of the wall. When pressure-washing wood, select the nozzle that will clean the wood with the minimum amount of pressure. Maintain a greater distance between the nozzle and the wood to help prevent splintering the wood.

Chapter 17 | Exterior Repairs

GUTTERS AND DOWNSPOUTS

SKILL LEVEL

- Semiskilled

TOOLS REQUIRED

- Extension ladder
- Tape measure
- Four-way screwdriver
- Cordless drill
- Hacksaw
- 2-foot level

MATERIALS REQUIRED

- Replacement gutter screws and ferrules
- Hidden gutter brackets
- 10-foot length of 2 x 3-inch downspout
- Spillways
- Gutter seam kit
- Gutter sealant
- Self-tapping screws

Gutter and downspout maintenance can be the difference between a dry basement or a damp basement. In addition, it can prevent damage, both seen and unseen, to the building foundation's structural integrity. Note: When attempting to check the roof gutters or elevated downspouts, use extreme caution and proper ladders. Perform the work when someone is home to assist you in case of an accident. An elderly experienced carpenter I know broke his hip from a ladder fall while cleaning his gutters when he was the only one at home.

First, inspect the condition of the gutters. Are they in sound shape with no holes, leaky seams, or clogs that could cause them to overflow during rainstorms? A common problem with older gutters is that they were made in only 10- or 20-foot lengths and were joined together using a gutter seam piece, rivets, and gutter sealant. During many years of seasonal changes, the gutter sealant would become brittle and cracked or the gutters would rot where the gutter seams were joined together. Since the 1970s, gutters have been made from seamless aluminum in continuous lengths up to 300 feet, eliminating the need for seams in repeating 10- or 20-foot sections.

Gutters also must have the proper pitch or slope from the closed end to the point of discharge into the vertical downspouts. Slope that ranges from ⅛ to ¼ inch per foot of gutter is acceptable to properly drain a 5-inch K-style or half-round gutter.

The way that gutters are attached to the building varies with the age of the gutter, and most styles are still available today. The oldest style of gutter is the half-round style, with corrugated round downspouts. These gutters require a three-piece attachment system. A metal vertical attachment piece with holes to set the slope of the gutter correctly is attached to the roof or the fascia boards. A half-round bracket is screwed to the vertical attachment piece with a round-head slotted screw and a square nut. Finally, a pre-bent wire piece is attached to the half-round bracket after the gutter is in place to secure the gutter to the assembled metal brackets.

The most common gutter used today is the K-style gutter. K-style gutters were originally attached with a spike-and-ferrule fastening system. The spike is nailed through the face of the gutter front, through the ferrule, and into the ends of the roof rafters or trusses behind the fascia boards.

The ferrule is extremely important because it prevents the gutter from collapsing as the spike is nailed tight. Any spikes that become loose and stick out can be tapped back in tight using a hammer.

Tap loose spikes back in with a hammer.

REPLACING GUTTER SCREWS OR FERRULES

If a spike is missing or a ferrule is damaged, you can purchase a pack of new gutter screws and ferrules from the home-supply center.

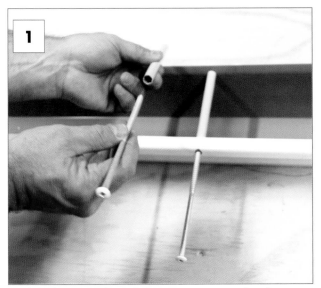

1 Slide the screw through the new or existing ferrule.

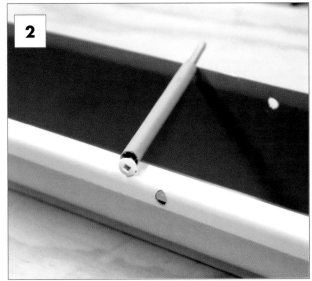

2 Use a cordless drill with a #2 square drive bit to turn the screw into the existing fascia board behind the gutter. The screw threads are larger in diameter than the original nail spike to ensure that it grabs.

K-STYLE GUTTERS

Since the mid 1980s, K-style gutters have been attached with a hidden-bracket-and-screw system to replace the original spike-and-ferrule system. The hidden bracket can be used in conjunction with an existing spike and ferrule that will not remain tight.

1 Insert the bracket into the front lip of the K-style gutter beside the loose spike and ferrule.

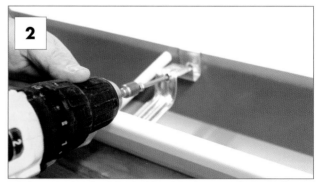

2 Place the back of the hidden bracket over the top of the back edge of the K-style gutter. Use a cordless screwdriver and a ¼-inch hex bit in the drill. Make sure the gutter is positioned properly and tighten the hidden bracket screw.

GUTTER END CAPS

Older gutter end caps are notorious for leaks, especially on the low end, where the downspout drop is located. Water collects at this end if the downspout is clogged, which allows water to dam up against the end cap. The gutter seam material can be missing, which causes leaks.

1 Cleaning the area and adding gutter seal material can help eliminate leaks.

GUTTER SEAMS

Old gutter seams require attention if they are leaky. Sometimes you just need to apply additional gutter seal material to the inside of the gutter after cleaning the area; other times, you will need to install a new gutter seam.

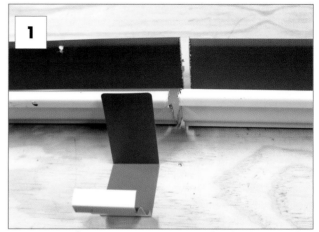

1 Cut apart the existing gutter seam with a hacksaw and remove the metal seam and gutter seal material.

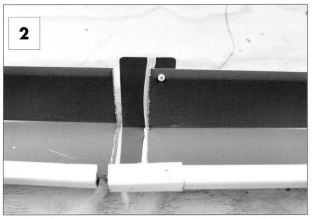

2 Place the new gutter seam material over one end of the existing gutter and install gutter seal material between the two before attaching with the two screws.

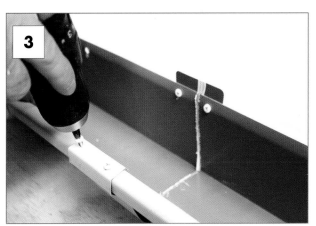

3 Place the gutter seal material on the remaining gutter and gutter seam material half and attach the other side of the joint with the two screws.

4 Apply additional gutter seal material on the inside, where the splice is, and you can add some to the outside of the gutter seam if the sealant matches the gutter color; otherwise, use clear silicone on the outside. Allow the seal material to dry thoroughly before the next rain event.

DOWNSPOUT REPAIR

Maintaining good downspout joint connections is important to the overall maintenance of the gutter system. When downspout sections need to be replaced, be sure to assemble the pieces correctly.

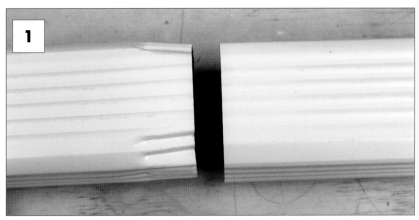

1 Each end of the spout has two configurations: one is tapered and the other is straight.

Gutters and Downspouts

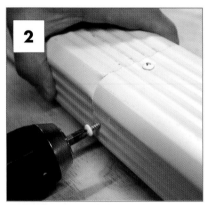

2 For future repairs or maintenance, self-tapping screws are best. Be sure to install one screw in the 3-inch face and one in the 2-inch side of the downspout just below the top edge of the seam and screw tight to secure.

3 A downspout termination at the bottom, where you can use a 4-inch round, thin-wall PVC pipe to direct the water either underground or across the ground, is important. The adapter fitting has to match both the PVC pipe diameter and the downspout size. Be sure to cut the last downspout long enough to fit securely into the top of the adapter. Dry-fit the length before attaching the two screws at the last downspout seam.

4 The discharge end of the PVC pipe may require a fitting to direct the water in a certain direction. Shown is a 45-degree elbow to direct the water down the side of the driveway. The fitting also helps add strength to the end of the pipe.

5 Vertical downspouts have many options to properly discharge the rainwater away from the foundation and prevent rainwater from seeping back against the building's foundation.

6 Option 1: Discharge rainwater onto the ground through a short section of downspout with proper grade sloping away from the home. With this option, the end of the aluminum downspout may become crushed, which slows the discharge rate of the rainwater.

7 Damaged downspout ends can be repaired using a hacksaw with a metal cutting blade. Square a cut line around the downspout, place the piece on an elevated surface like a bucket or saw horse, and carefully cut the damaged end off.

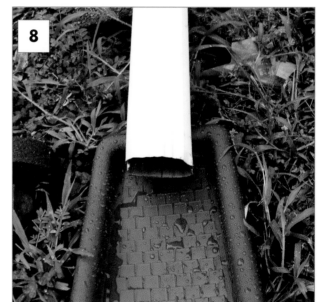

8 Option 2: Discharge rainwater onto a spillway made of plastic or concrete through a short section of downspout with proper grade sloping away from the house. The advantage of placing a spillway on the ground is that it keeps the ground from being saturated with rainwater. It also gives the person mowing the lawn a reminder to stop and remove the downspout extension and the spillway or to use a string trimmer to trim the grass around the spillway.

9 Option 3: Discharge rainwater from the downspout into a rigid PVC or flexible corrugated PVC pipe with a spout adapter. The discharge of rainwater will drain with proper grade sloping away from the house.

Areas of the lawn that collect rainwater discharge and runoff may create other issues that can be corrected by using a plastic yard drain inlet box, piping, fittings, and spillways. You can purchase these items inexpensively at most any home-supply center. Using the provided instructions to determine which side(s) of the inlet box will have pipe access, you can easily design the system to create a way for collected water to be piped underground and discharge onto an area of the yard that permits better gravity flow or is in a more acceptable place.

In the photo to the right, driveway water runoff combined with rainwater downspout discharge can collect between two properties near a solid wooden fence. A section of 4-inch pipe underground, along with the plastic yard drain inlet box, allows the water to discharge in a larger rear yard area.

Chapter 17 | Exterior Repairs

MAILBOXES

SKILL LEVEL

- Basic

TOOLS REQUIRED

- Pencil
- Tape measure
- Four-way screwdriver
- Hammer
- Cordless drill and twist bits
- Circular saw

MATERIALS REQUIRED

- New mailbox (post- or wall-mounted)
- Small piece of wood
- Exterior wood screws
- Masonry anchors (if mounting on stucco, stone, or brick)

Mailboxes mounted on posts take a lot of abuse compared to those mounted on houses. In almost every movie ever made about rambunctious teenagers, there is always a scene involving a car, a baseball bat, and a mailbox on a post. Yep, you guessed it—the bat survived, but the mailbox didn't. (Reminds me of a time in the early 70's in a small town somewhere that involved some teenagers, maybe a mailbox and the police? I think it's just all made up—at least that's my story and I'm sticking to it!)

Another mailbox catastrophe is when the snowplow driver misjudges the edge of the road, and the force of the plowed snow knocks the mailbox right over like a bowling pin! Actually if you call the municipality, they can inform you about getting reimbursed for the snow plowing over your box. I think you have to show that the plow ran past the edge of the road.

The United States Postal Service regulates the use of and specifications regarding mailboxes. You may need to repair or replace your mailbox to be compliant for mail delivery.

The most common type of mailbox is either plastic or metal, mounted to a wooden post. The mailbox must be a specific height. In some housing developments, all of the mailboxes are in a cluster rather than each home having an individual box at the end of the driveway. In order for the mail carrier to pick up mail from the box, a red flag is raised in the vertical position.

Each mailbox is required to have the house number somewhere on the box to assure accurate mail delivery.

Other mailbox styles include the wall-mounted version for the front of the home. There is also a lockable type of box to help safeguard your incoming mail. The disadvantage is that the outgoing mail has to be visible sticking out of the mailbox top as the postal carrier will not have a key to access the mail inside. The big advantage to using this style of box is in cities and larger townhome communities where the postal carrier delivers mail by walking door to door.

POST-MOUNTED MAILBOX REPAIR

Replacing a plastic post-mounted mailbox or the wood it is attached to is very easy. Remove the existing mailbox and the deteriorated wood to which the box is mounted. The new plastic mailbox will require a wooden post with different measurements.

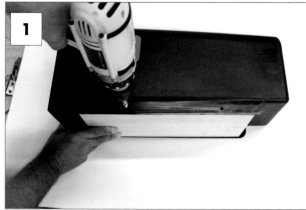

1 Place the new wood piece in the recessed bottom of the new plastic mailbox and attach the wood with new exterior wood screws through the existing holes.

2 Unscrew and remove the wood piece from the recess of the bottom of the mailbox and attach the wood piece to the top of existing post. Reattach the screws through the same side holes previously installed.

WALL-MOUNTED MAILBOX REPAIR

A metal wall-mounted mailbox can require you to assemble the parts, which include the box, lockset, lock-retaining clip, key, and MAIL emblem.

Chapter 17 | Exterior Repairs

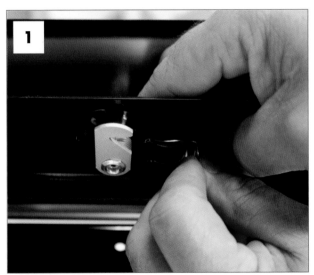

1 Follow the instructions on the box to insert the lock into the hole in the mail slot flap and attach the lock-retaining clip.

2 Cut the installation instructions along the dotted line to use as a drill marking template on the exterior wall.

3 Place a mark at a maximum of 5 feet above the floor surface below to locate the top of the instructions. Mark the holes on the exterior wall by poking a hole in the center of the circle on the instructions. For wood or vinyl siding, use a drill bit to start the hole at 50 percent of the screw diameter.

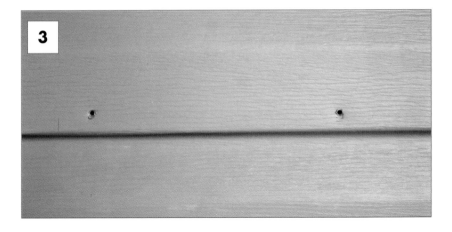

✓ TIP

The mailbox does not come with mounting screws. Because the outside wall material can be wood or vinyl siding, requiring wood screws to attach. If the exterior wall can be brick, concrete, or stone, it will require ¼-inch plastic masonry anchors that will secure the screws in the anchors.

Chapter 17 | Exterior Repairs

Mailboxes

4 Turn the MAIL emblem over, remove the paper from the four pieces of double-sided tape, and place the emblem on the front of the mailbox.

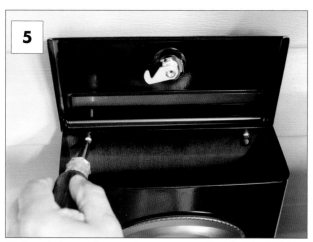

5 Attach the mailbox to the exterior wall with two screws (see previous mounting screw note) and tighten with a Phillips-head screwdriver. Close the mail slot flap and turn the key to lock and remove the key.

The mail will be delivered through the mail slot under the mailbox lid by the mail person. You can access the mail by unlocking the mail slot flap. Caution: For outgoing mail, it is advisable to place your mail in a daily collection box provided by the US Postal Service. Placing mail inside a mailbox with a red flag or so that it sticks out of the metal mailbox lid is an invitation to others.

In addition to marking the mailbox with the house number, the house number should also be attached to the front of the house or building so deliveries arrive to the correct location. Many municipalities support the idea of each house having a double-sided reflective house number on a post in the front yard that is easily visible to emergency responders to cut down on response time to the correct location. These numbers may be provided at cost by the local fire department or township office.

OUTDOOR LIGHTS

SKILL LEVEL

- **Semiskilled**

TOOLS REQUIRED

- **Four-way screwdriver**
- **Stepladder**
- **Nut driver**
- **Torpedo level**

MATERIALS REQUIRED

- **New fixture**
- **New light bulbs**

Outdoor light fixtures require maintenance in the form of cleaning and light-bulb replacement. They may need to be replaced if the weather elements take their toll on the finish and other parts of the fixtures, or if they stop working.

Outdoor light fixtures may stop working or a variety of reasons. The best way to troubleshoot is to work from the simplest to the hardest tasks. Don't assume the fixture isn't working just because it is old. I have worked around light fixtures older than me, if you can believe that, and they perform flawlessly every day. (Although I have yet to come across a working light bulb older than me!)

First, check to see if the light bulb is tight in the socket. A loose bulb can act the same as a blown bulb. Remove the bulb and, if it is an incandescent light bulb, shake it to see if you hear a rattle of the elements. If so, replace it with a new bulb and turn the light switch on.

Second, check the breaker or fuse to which the light circuit is connected. It is possible that the light is connected to something else that caused a short in the circuit, and the breaker tripped or the fuse blew. Reset the breaker or replace the blown fuse and turn the light switch on. If the circuit shorts again, it is time to call a qualified electrician.

Third, turn the power off at the breaker or fuse.

1 Remove the light bulb and unscrew the fasteners that attach the light fixture to the box.

Chapter 17 | Exterior Repairs

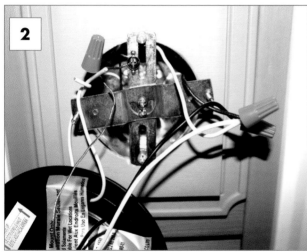

2 Use a piece of wire through one mounting hole and connect it to the cross bar of the light fixture to support the light fixture while you check the wire connections between the light fixture and the house.

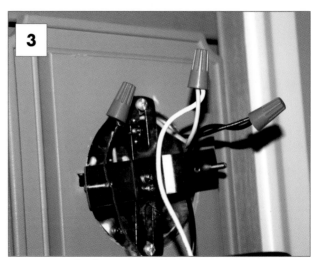

3 Separate the three wires—black, white, and ground—to complete a thorough inspection of each.

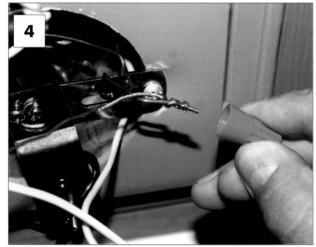

4 Unscrew the wire nut caps of each wire to be sure that the stranded wires of the light fixture and the solid wire of the house wires are making good contact with each other. Older light fixture wires can become brittle from the heat of the light bulb. If these wire connections are good, chances are the light fixture is suspect and needs replacing.

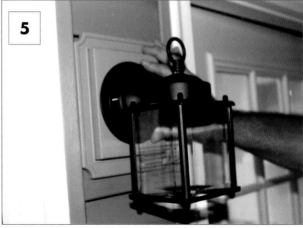

5 The new fixture will include a new cross bar and mounting studs. Be sure to use these, as the old parts may be corroded from outside moisture that has worked its way into the junction box. Follow the manufacturer's instructions on assembling the light fixture and installing it. Also use the new wire nut caps that come with the fixture for the best electrical connections. Install the new fixture over the mounting studs threaded into the cross bar and install the fastening hardware to secure the light fixture to the junction box. Be sure to use a torpedo level to set the bottom of the light fixture horizontal. Install a 60-watt or lower bulb (not included with the fixture). Be sure the bulb is secured tightly for a good connection. Turn the power back on at the breaker or fuse location and then turn on the switch to the outdoor light. Bingo! The light will be on.

OUTDOOR GFCI RECEPTACLE COVERS

SKILL LEVEL

- Semiskilled

TOOLS REQUIRED

- Four-way screwdriver

MATERIALS REQUIRED

- New spring-loaded receptacle cover plate and gasket set or new in-use cover plate and gasket set

When an outdoor receptacle is used, it must include an approved watertight outdoor receptacle cover plate. The cover plates are available in two versions.

1. A spring-loaded watertight cover plate with gaskets that seal the receptacle insert prongs. This type of cover does *not* provide watertight protection when the plug is in the receptacle, as the plug holds the spring-loaded cover open.
2. In-use watertight cover plates allow for the extension cord or device power cord to exit the bottom of the cover and provide watertight conditions for the receptacle.

Receptacles for outdoor power cord connections are required to be ground fault circuit interrupter (GFCI) protected circuits. This can be accomplished by one of three methods.

1. The circuit is powered by a GFCI breaker in the main electrical panel box.
2. The circuit is powered by a GFCI-controlled receptacle inside or outside the building
3. The circuit is powered by an individual GFCI receptacle outside the building.

Spring-loaded cover plate.

In-use cover plates.

REPLACING SPRING-LOADED COVER

In every case, the GFCI receptacle or breaker that controls the receptacle circuit being used has to be reset if the circuit detects a fault to the circuit. This is what protects the user from electrical hazards but *not* from electrocution. To replace an outdoor spring-loaded cover, you need to purchase a new one of the same type. These covers can be mounted vertically, as shown here (right), or horizontally.

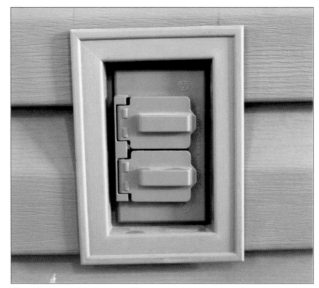

Vertically mounted spring-loaded cover.

1 Remove the center screw that attaches the cover plate from the receptacle device.

2 Remove the old weathertight foam gasket and install the new one. Be sure to remove the cover-plate gaskets from the foam sheet before you discard it. Install the new spring-loaded cover plate, making sure the gasket pieces also fit into the covers. This will ensure that water does not seep into the receptacle device when it is not in use, causing an electrical short.

Outdoor GFCI Receptacle Covers

REPLACING IN-USE COVER

1 To replace an in-use outdoor cover, use the same method as previously described. To properly use an in-use outdoor receptacle cover, you first must locate the locking tab. Press the tab so it disengages the lock bump at the corner of the cover. Swing the door open to access the receptacle. Plug in the electrical device or the outdoor-approved extension cord. Route the electrical cord through the appropriate wire slot on the cover extension. Close the in-use cover and engage the lock tab to keep the door closed, protecting the cord connection being used.

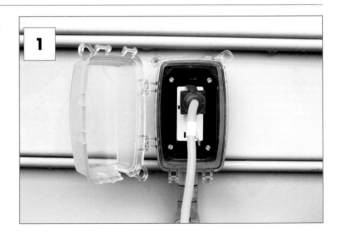

WOODEN DECK RAILS

SKILL LEVEL

- Semiskilled

TOOLS REQUIRED

- Pencil
- Tape measure
- Nail puller
- Hammer
- Speed square
- Permanent marker
- Scribe
- Circular saw
- Cordless drill with magnetic bit extension
- Electric drill and twist bits
- Extension cord

MATERIALS REQUIRED

- Replacement exterior wood
- 2½-inch exterior coated deck screws

Wooden deck rails can withstand a lot of exposure to weather changes when they are made of pressure-treated wood, cedar, or redwood. These materials are intended to be outdoors for all four seasons.

Even the best wood for exterior use will eventually break down, warp, bow, cup, or twist. Yet, with careful planning, material selection, and installation techniques, you can replace the damaged wood, and the new wood will last as long as, if not longer than, the original wood. This is due in part to improvements in the materials, higher-quality fasteners, and better installation methods used today.

1 For the T-style top rail, locate all of the nails holding the top piece in place. Using a nail puller (referred to as a "cat's paw"), place the slotted head of the tool beside the common nail head. Strike the head of the nail puller and at the same time rotate the handle vertically. The hammer action will allow the jaws of the nail puller to embed into the wood and then, when rotated, grab the head of the nail.

2 When you pull on the handle in a downward motion, the head of the nail rises up from the top surface of the wood. Remove all of the nails holding the top T-piece and set aside.

3 Next, using a circular saw with a 7¼-inch-diameter blade, set the blade depth to 1½ inches. Cut the top T-board across the face and be sure not to cut the vertical board under the top T-rail if necessary to remove. Note: Because wood shrinks, it may not be necessary to cut the top rail in two to remove it. Remove the top T-rail and begin the process of installing the replacement board. Start with a board that is longer than the old board. Set one end of the board against one of the two posts between which the board has to be cut. Make sure that the other end is centered and resting on top of the opposite post.

4 By using the square as a straightedge, ensure that the edge of the board is flush with the face of the post.

Chapter 17 | Exterior Repairs

5 Since most wooden posts will twist over time, check with a square to see if the inside edge of the post is square with the vertical T-rail.

6 If there are any gaps along the side of the post and the square, you will need to scribe the end of the new board to match the twist of the post; otherwise, the square end of the board will leave an unwanted gap.

7 Use a marker, pen, pencil, or carpenter scribe to mark the board end parallel to the first post. Cut the board at this line only and recheck the cut for accuracy against the first post.

8 When the final cut of the scribed end matches the twist angle of the face of the post, there will not be any gaps. We have to keep the board oriented in the way it fits best to make all of the final measurements.

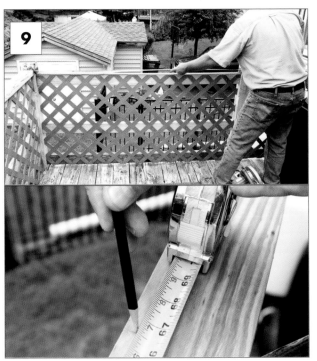

10 Mark both dimensions along the top face of the new T-rail board and use a straightedge to connect the two measurement marks. In almost all cases, the line will not be square to the board edge because the posts twisted from the original installation.

9 Measure the distance between the first and second posts on the outside as well as on the inside of the posts. Record the dimensions on a piece of paper or on top of the vertical board under the top T-rail. In this case, the F measurement, or front, is toward you, and the R measurement, or rear, is away from you when looking down on the board to measure and mark for cutting.

11 Place an X on the scrap side of the cut line, assuring that the saw blade kerf thickness passes on that side of the line. In doing so, it does *not* make your cut board too short. Dry-fit the board between the two posts to ensure a correct fit

12 If the board is too long, mark the amount of excess material with a line on the board end of your second cut. Use a circular saw with the motor over the long end of the board for better balance and cut accuracy. Use a tapping block if the board will go into place but needs a little help from a hammer.

Chapter 17 | Exterior Repairs

13 When the board fits as desired, mark and predrill clearance holes through the center of the top face of the board. This ensures that the ceramic-coated screws properly attach themselves into the top edge of the vertical board under the T-rail. *Do not drill too deep, as the screws will not have holding power.* For an 8-foot-long rail, I drilled five screw holes in the top rail, with the end ones 7 inches from each end.

14 Also predrill holes in each of the four edges of the T-rail ends to provide for additional attachment to the posts and prevent twisting of the top T-rail.

15 Using a magnetic screw starter tip, install the ceramic screws into the top T-rail predrilled holes and then tighten them until the tops of the flat-head screws are flush with the top of the board. If set too high, the screws can snag things; if set too deep, the screws will cause the board to rot faster. An 8-foot top rail required nine screws: five in the top face and one in each of the board edges at the ends. When you've completed the top rail replacement, it will look very clean and professionally done.

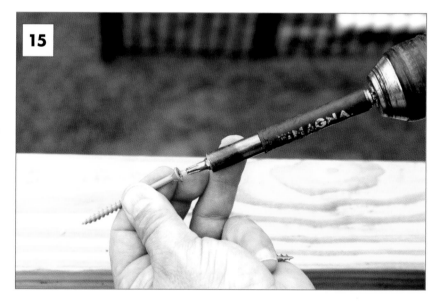

ACKNOWLEDGMENTS

To acknowledge the influence of so many in my construction career who provided me with knowledge, insight, and experience is very important to the creation of this book. Without these people taking an interest in a guy who was originally trained in the field of tool and machine design and not construction cannot be understated.

My brothers Phillip and Tom were very instrumental in my earliest years when building my first home in 1982, in which I still reside, and for giving me moral support as my construction career grew into a full-time business of building new homes and renovating existing ones.

Thank you to the colleagues and subcontractors in the building industry who worked with my schedules, ideas, and customers' needs during some of the tough economic times in the 1990s to create some of the nicest homes a small-town small business could design and build.

Thank you to my colleagues at Thaddeus Stevens College of Technology, where I am an assistant professor of residential remodeling technology, for working with me over the past fifteen years to train young men and women of the Commonwealth of Pennsylvania to become the best building and remodeling craftspeople who will lead the next generation of workers.

I want to acknowledge the many friendships that have come through the years since I first started swinging a hammer and working my way through the building trade in 1982. Nothing can be more satisfying than, when the end of the day comes, to look back at the site and see that what is there now was not yet there yesterday!

ART CREDITS

ABOUT THE AUTHOR

Charles T. Byers is a 1979 graduate of Thaddeus Stevens College of Technology, where he received an associate's degree in Mechanical Drafting and Design. During his work as a mechanical design engineer, he worked on many major projects for Fortune 500 companies, including contracts with the U.S. Postal Service, Harley-Davidson, and Caterpillar. In 1982 he began his construction career by building his own residence. In 1997 he received an FHA/VA Builder's Certificate and has constructed over 25 new homes and countless remodeling projects during his building career.

In 2003 he became an Instructor in the Carpentry Technology department at Thaddeus Stevens College of Technology, where he instructed students to build 25 residences in the city of Lancaster, PA. In 2015 he became an Assistant Professor in the Residential Remodeling Technology department, teaching students every aspect of home remodeling and repairs.

In 2017 he is credited as the Technical Editor for several Creative Homeowner books: *Ultimate Guide to Home Repairs*, *Ultimate Guide to Wiring*, and *Ultimate Guide to Plumbing*. He resides in Conestoga, PA, near his two daughters, eight grandchildren, and one great-grandson.

INDEX